IT'S POSSIBLE:

LIVING BEYOND LIMITATIONS!

Andrea L. Dudley

Habakkuk Publishing

Canton, Michigan

Habakkuk Publishing

P.O. Box 871074

Canton, Michigan 48188

www.globalempact.org/habakkuk_publishing

No part of this book may be reproduced, stored in a retrieval system, or transmitted by any means without the written permission of the author.

First Published by Habakkuk Publishing; 6/19/2012

ISBN: 978-097980822-7

Printed in the United States of America

This book is printed on acid-free paper.

Unless otherwise identified, Scripture references are taken from the King James Version of the Holy Bible.

For more information or additional copies, go to:
www.globalempact.org/habakkuk_publishing

Habakkuk Publishing
734.772.2079
habakkukstories@yahoo.com

Dedication

This book is dedicated to the memory of my dear mother, Vera M. Beard, who went to be with the Lord on March 13, 2012. She was quite, yet strong; reserved, yet engaged! Her children were the center of her affection, her attention and her life. I often wondered what Mom's hobbies and true interests were…and of course, it was us…her children. She was totally and completely dedicated to nurturing all four of her children. Mom, you are missed today more than yesterday; and I am sure that, as the days pass by, I'll only miss you more. But I'm also comforted by the fact that I know the Lord has called you home to enter into your eternal rest.

Acknowledgments

I have been exceptionally blessed to have married Michael Thomas Dudley. We celebrated 30 years of wedded bliss on October 3, 2011. He has been my rock, my strength, my encourager and my friend…and, as always, he cheered me on to victory. He has always supported me and constantly tells me that I'm a good woman. I appreciate him for inspiring me to live out my dreams and for never, ever releasing negative words over me. It's Michael who should get the credit for any success that I've attained…for because of him, I am able to be me.

Also, our wonderful youngest son, Solomon, has been and is my ever-present helper and "personal assistant." Without his help, my life would certainly be more challenging.

Contents

Introduction

Courageous is the one word that can be used to describe each of the contributing authors featured in **It's Possible: Living Beyond Limitations!** It takes courage to look cancer in the eye and say, "I will live and I will not die." It takes courage to leave an abusive marriage when all of your "Christian" friends are saying that you "have to stay." And, it takes courage to defy cultural myths to leave what is familiar and venture out into a world of the unknown…a world that holds the life of your dreams. Our nineteen co-authors have done this…and more. They are: Rev. Dr. Peninnah M. Kako, Judith S. Cooper, Amy J. Meyer-Johnson, Rev. Helene Walker, Apostle Londen Winders, Michele Sweeting Decaro, Linda A. Haywood, Rebecca Bailey, Zabrina Gordon, Caroline D. Parker, Minister Mary Edwards, Carolyn Solomon, Evangelist Valerie M. Robinson, Pastor O. Agnes Kgasoe, Linda Jo White, Cynthia Moore, Pastor Kimberly Brown, Faith Larkins and Kisha Emanuel Durrell. Against all odds, they have conquered mental illness and destroyed the effects of sexual abuse and abortion. They have not allowed their circumstances to defeat, define or deny them their destiny. These women are champions, and we salute each author!

It's Possible: Living Beyond Limitations! inspires, encourages, and empowers women to rise to the fullness of their potential. Each woman has written a powerful story of how she overcame a limitation imposed upon her…because of a health issue, a broken relationship, financial difficulties, or some other life-wrenching challenge. The authors' moving stories motivate women to stand tall and successfully surmount the myriad of challenges they have faced! It is encouraging to know that ordinary women have achieved extraordinary results through faith in the power of God's Word. These authors are influential speakers, educators, entrepreneurs, pastors and leaders. Their electrifying stories will inspire you to move closer to the heartbeat of God's master plan for your life.

One of my favorite scriptures is Philippians 4:13: "I can do all things through Christ who strengthens me." This scripture is my life mantra…it fuels my passion to live out my dreams. No matter what limitations you may face, we hope that, after reading this anthology, you too will realize that there is nothing you cannot achieve. If you're in a race, run harder! If you're on the side-lines, get back in the race. Be encouraged. Enjoy.

THE POWER OF THE WORD AND VISION

Rev. Dr. Peninnah M. Kako, PhD

My story is that of divine grace, favor, and love by a God that would rather die than spend an eternity without me. I feel truly honored by such love and thank my Heavenly Father and my Lord Jesus Christ for His grace and mercy. The reason I am so appreciative is that, while growing up, I could never have imagined in my natural mind that my life could turn out as it has. I was born and raised in rural eastern Kenya. My mother always struggled to make ends meet—in fact, the ends never met. In those days, it was common to have no food, but somehow we seemed contented.

My Mother loved the Lord. Most nights, she would sit the children down to tell them stories and read scriptures. I am the 5th out of a family of nine. I remember the late evenings when, while waiting for our food to be ready, my mother would have us memorize comforting scriptures that gave us hope for a better future. John 14:1 was one of those scriptures. I can still hear her voice as she led my siblings and me into repeating choruses so that we could remember them—singing together into the night. "Let not your heart be troubled, you believe in Me, believe also in God." Little did I know that these same words were seeds planted in my spirit. At that time, it was not obvious to us, but my mother was simply using the scriptures to keep us focused on having a better life than we had. God used these moments to plant seeds of hope in my life. I began to notice gender-based injustices towards women rooted in the traditional norms that I did not like. I had witnessed that women were, as a way of life and expectation, counted as subservient to the men in the community—and I did not understand why. I just knew that I wanted a better life.

Life changed forever

On the day that I accepted Jesus Christ as my Savior, my life changed forever. At 14 years old, I was preparing to go to boarding high school. I had gone to the market for no apparent reason, but little did I know that this would be "my day." I met my classmate there, who presented to me the simple gospel of salvation and asked me to respond to it. I did respond—and that was the beginning of real change and hope in my life. In a few weeks, I was filled with the Holy Spirit and a new life began to spring from my heart. I just knew within my spirit that I was meant to do more—to be different. God made a way and I was admitted to a boarding school 400 miles away from my village—a place where I would meet people from every province in Kenya. Here, God began to teach me His Word, I started leading a Bible study and began to grow in God.

Saying no to poverty and cultural barriers

> *"For with God nothing is ever impossible and no Word from God shall be without power or impossible of fulfillment." Luke 1:37, AMP*

At this time, all I wanted was more of God. I was so hungry for the truth that when a friend informed me that the only people going to heaven were Seventh Day Adventists, I became one. It lasted one semester, but I soon found out that only faith in Jesus and His saving grace was necessary. Even during that time, God was still faithful. By His grace, I was able to block poverty at home so that I could focus on doing well in class. I liked my school but there was one problem—I didn't have the tuition. Although it bothered me that I didn't know what would happen, I kept my focus on school and Jesus. I had hope.

I had hope because I did not want to be poor. I knew if I could just get my education and go to college, then I would not have to be subservient, as were the expectations from the village. I did not truly know what having faith meant, but I knew, from the stories my mother told, that there was hope in God. You see, my father passed away when I was nine, and by the neighbors' assessments, I was destined to drop out of school and become a "housemaid." In low-income counties such as Kenya, education is an avenue for a better life. My family situation was threatening my only road to a better future.

After I found the Lord, I began to read scriptures and discovered that Jesus loves me. My Bible became my escape from poverty. The more I put God as the center in my life, favor came to me. God touched the hearts of the school authorities and they paid my tuition. God gave me success academically. When I completed high school, my village clan did not support my continued education. They believed that girls should not be educated because they will be married off to become a "housemaid." At that time, students were required to attend two years of advanced level schooling after high school before they could be admitted to the university. So—I believed God. He made a way and I sailed through my years of advanced level education and went on to the University in Kenya. This was a really big achievement for a village girl with a big dream.

The power of image

Looking back, I now realize that inner strength, courage, a dependency on God, and a mental image of success were key to breaking these first set points in my life. I constantly entertained thoughts of hope and success. I just knew that God would provide whatever I needed—and He did. I knew that God wanted my mind to be filled with His thoughts, according to Romans 12:2.

To develop the vision of breaking off from prevailing gender roles and poverty, I chose to focus on the Word of God. He began to give me thoughts of meeting people of different color and race. My older sister worked for foreigners, and she would often send my mother magazines with pictures of people from different parts of the world, especially America. I was very fascinated by the people and began to cut out the pictures and paste them around my mother's living room. I would imagine myself having conversations with these people that I had never known. I later realized that God was allowing me to create a vision in my mind for what was to come. What is amazing about that is, at the time, I did not know God was renewing my mind so that I could accept what was to come later. I had a great hunger for the things of God—for his Word. I now know that, when we plant the seed of God's Word in our spirits, He works in us even though our natural senses might not be aware of it. By meditating on the Scriptures and entertaining a visionary mindset, my life began to change.

Right place at the right time

One day while preparing to go to college, I met my cousin who lived in U.S. He had come to visit Kenya on his vacation. He quickly commented that he had a friend in the U.S. who would like to meet me. I brushed him off. My focus was on college and on my salvation. Later, I came to marry that friend of his—my husband John. I learned that when we put God first, He takes care of the details in our

lives. It was 1987 and I was 22 years old. After 11 months of waiting to join my husband in the U.S., God again opened a door and I received my visa.
Hoping to continue my education, I applied to a university. They turned me down because my grades were not good enough. I decided to go for an associate degree and continue my pursuit. For the most part, I simply wanted Jesus to be the center of everything I sought to do.

Coming from Kenya, I had a negative view of religion—because when I was newly born-again, I was in a denominational church that did not believe in the power of the Holy Spirit. I was hungry for all God had for me and had received the baptism of the Holy Spirit. Because of this, I was excommunicated from the church. But since that time, my faith in Jesus has been central to everything I do. God knew my heart's desires, and after joining my husband, I was privileged to sit under some wonderful pastors—now Apostles Michael and Andrea Dudley—from 1993-2001. This was a divine connection. During that time, I grew more spiritually and learned to serve others.

Dream come true

God has so graciously blessed me with a wonderful husband and two God-fearing sons, Joseph, who is 22, and Paul, who is 21. In addition to enjoying my wonderful family, by the grace and favor of God, in 2003, I began my pursuit for a doctoral education. My dissertation proved to be one of the most difficult things I had ever attempted. I again applied the Word and Vision. I cut out scriptures, such as: "I have more understanding than all my teachers, for your testimonies are my meditation." (Psalms 119:99 ESV) "For I can do everything through Christ, who gives me strength." (Philippians 4:13 NLT) "For nothing will be impossible with God." (Luke 1:37 ESV). I posted these scriptures in my work area and included a future date I intended to defend. With the Word and Vision at work, in June 2008, I successfully defended my dissertation—one month from the date I had initially posted. In addition, I completed my PhD in Nursing without any loan, all because of God's Word—graduating from the same university that initially turned me down. He not only made a way for me, He made a highway for my success. His nature is always to do exceedingly abundantly above all that we can ask or think (Ephesians 3: 20). Furthermore, He has given my husband and me a Ministry with a Global Vision, committed to connecting all people to Christ. Surely, what God can do, no one else can do; when God says "yes," no one can say "no." In my life I have faced many obstacles, but I have also learned the power of the Word and Vision. The Word and Vision have the power to bring things that are not seen into the "seen" realm—by faith. When I made a conscious decision to partner with Jesus, He opened doors that nobody else could open. The set points in my life only served as punctuations to glorify God throughout the pages of my life—with the WORD and VISION, I am a witness—it is possible!

FREED FROM BONDAGE

Linda A. Haywood

The National Alliance on Mental Illness (NAMI) defines mental illness as a medical condition that disrupts a person's thinking, feeling, mood and ability to relate to others. Looking back, mental illness was not a term that I ever heard of or understood as I was growing up. I knew about "those crazy people" who frequently walked up and down the streets in our community, unkempt and usually laughing or talking to themselves. Some were considered a nuisance. Others were considered dangerous. None were considered as "normal people" experiencing a medical condition. As I grew up shunning "those people," little did I know that one day I would be used to combat many of the myths and stigmas attached to mental illness.

As a child, I had always envisioned myself being a normal wife with a fantastic career and a husband who made lots of money so that we could afford a nice home with three bedrooms, roses adorning our yard, two white French poodles and a two or three car garage. But my life turned out to be anything but normal.

In retrospect, I always felt there was "something wrong" with me but I didn't know how to articulate my experience. By the time I reached puberty, I was prone to terrifying nightmares, and I had hallucinations, as well as auditory hallucinations in which I would hear others whispering and laughing—even when I was at home alone. And, since I was often bullied by my peers and had few friends, I stayed very depressed and frequently wrestled with thoughts of suicide.

However, I would have never imagined that I was "crazy" or mentally ill. Even when I thought of questioning my behavior, I wouldn't have expected or accepted that I was experiencing a mental illness. At that time, most people, including myself, equated someone having a mental illness with someone having a deficit in intelligence. The fact that I stayed on the honor roll was enough to convince myself, and everyone else concerned about me, that I was just fine—and would stay that way.

At the age of 21, I was a new wife and mother of an eight-month-old son when I was first admitted to a psychiatric unit. Several weeks prior to that admission, I had had a miscarriage with my second child; so, as the years went by, doctors suspected that I may have been experiencing postpartum depression at that time. In 1982, however, "postpartum depression" was not a term that was regularly used. In 1982, I had never heard of an African American having a "nervous breakdown"—and I felt as though I was a big failure and disappointment to my family. I sobbed uncontrollably the night that I was admitted to Hackley Hospital's new psychiatric wing in Muskegon, Michigan. To my despair, it was not to be my last admission.

I spent a month at Hackley Hospital before being released. But two days later, I returned to Hackley Hospital—distraught and suicidal. I spent the next ten years battling mental illness. During that ten-year period, my marriage ended, I lost custody of both my children, and I attempted suicide on three different occasions. To make matters more complicated, I became addicted to alcohol and other drugs, and endured two abusive relationships that served to bring my self-esteem even lower.

I tried a number of support groups, medications and psychiatrists over that ten-year period, but nothing seemed to cure my illness and I became increasingly hopeless over the years. I became unable to hold a job or an apartment. In 1989, I was sent to Northville Regional Hospital and felt that I had finally hit the bottom of the barrel. After being there for over a month, the "experts" signed a piece of paper that seemed to seal my fate. Psychiatrists stated that my prognosis was poor—that I was suicidal and homicidal and would likely need to be institutionalized "as needed" to alleviate my symptoms. Upon discharge, I was sent to an Adult Foster Care Home—or group home, as many are called.

Today, as a professional, I can look back and see that I stayed in denial of my mental health issues and addictions. I often sabotaged my own recovery by self-medicating, stopping my prescribed medications without medical monitoring or calling area crisis lines—threatening to kill myself, but refusing to go into treatment to alleviate my symptoms. Finally, my family was forced to petition me into the hospital for treatment. This cyclical behavior occurred over and over again until it felt like a "normal" part of my life.

I accepted the prognosis assigned to me and felt that my life was surely over. I was 29 years old and felt that my life would never change. I had resigned myself to the fact that I would be stuck in this imprisonment of my mind for the remainder of my life.

But, in 1991, my life took a turn! I wish I could tell you the exact moment it happened, but I can only say that God did a new thing in my life. After ten years of dealing with grievous depression, shame and despair, I was simply tired of being tired. I found myself pleading with God to make me better or let me go—without expecting any real answer. To my surprise, I developed an earnest desire to be mentally healthy and rebuild my life. I became serious and active in my recovery by cooperating and working with the mental health professionals. I stopped using alcohol and other drugs and found the strength to live again. I began doing so well that I was able to get my psychiatrist to complete and send a form to Social Security that allowed me to become my own payee and in charge of my funds. Although I hadn't lived alone in 3 ½ years, and many thought I couldn't make it on my own, I moved into my own apartment! I left the group home, with three bags of clothes and $20 to my name, and moved about 15 miles away to Ypsilanti, Michigan. Each day, I was growing stronger—that is, each day until I fell in with an abusive boyfriend. After a year of his abuse, I finally found the strength to believe that I deserved to be treated better. I broke away from this person (who would be my last abusive boyfriend), but I was again uncertain of my destiny. In January 1994, I enrolled in Washtenaw Community College just to "pass the time."

Well, in 1995, I graduated from Washtenaw Community College with honors, an Associate's degree in Liberal Arts and a desire to change the world! In 1996, I entered Eastern Michigan University's Bachelor of Social Work program and graduated with honors and on the Dean's List in 1998. I then began working at the same battered women's shelter where I had previously fled to escape the abuse.

In 2003, I began Eastern Michigan University's Master of Social Work program and graduated in 2005, again with honors. I left employment at the shelter and went on to work at Community Mental Health—becoming a colleague of the same psychiatrist and social workers who had diagnosed me and assisted me with case management.

To God be the glory! I have been totally healed of the mental illness that once plagued my life on a daily basis. In the past 25 years, I haven't been a patient in a psychiatric unit. That's quite an accomplishment for a person who was once hospitalized every other month, usually days after being discharged from a psychiatric unit. I am now a Master's level social worker, and I've worked with many who are going through mental illness, domestic violence and alcohol and drug abuse. Although my children were never returned to me and remained with my parents until they reached adulthood, our relationship has been restored and I thank God for them and for my family. As a family, we have had challenges to overcome, but God has allowed us to persevere. I accepted God's calling on my life and I'm currently a licensed minister as well and an award-winning author. I often look back in awe and thank God every day that I have been set free from the bondage of mental illness.

The Elephant Rope

As a man was passing by the elephants, he suddenly stopped, confused by the fact that these huge creatures were being held by only a small rope tied to their front leg. No chains, no cages. It was obvious that the elephants could, at any time, break away from their bonds…but for some reason, they did not.

He saw a trainer nearby and asked why these animals just stood there and made no attempt to get away. "Well," the trainer said, "when they are very young and much smaller, we use the same size rope to tie them, and at that age, it's enough to hold them. Then, as they grow up, they are conditioned to believe that they cannot break away. They believe the rope can still hold them, so they never try to break free."

The man was amazed. The animals could, at any time, break free from their bonds; but because the elephants really believed that they couldn't break away, they were truly stuck right where they were.

So, just like the elephants, how many of us go through our life hanging on to a belief that we simply cannot do a certain thing…simply because we failed at it once before? Or, are we are too afraid to attempt it…thereby eliminating ourselves before we even try? There is a saying that goes like this: "Nothing beats a failure but a try." Failure is part of learning…and we should never give up because of the struggles in our life.

COURAGE TO ENDURE THE STORM

Zabrina Gordon

It is human nature to think that we know what is best for our lives. More times than not, we react first to life's events, and then we are displeased with the outcome. Finally, we settle down long enough to recognize that our emotions caused us to overreact to the situation and that God was in control all along. At one time or another, life's circumstances, problems and troubles have thrown us a curve ball that spins us around and knocks us to the ground. Learning to totally trust, have confidence, and be obedient to God when he prompts us to do something is often very challenging. However, Christians must remember our position in Christ Jesus and truly latch on to our new identities in Him. That gives us authority over the enemy. (Matthew 18:18)

In November 2006, the Holy Spirit prompted me to fast and pray because a storm was on the horizon. I remember simply saying, "Yes LORD." I began to prepare myself by forming a group of saints to be in prayer for me and by praying that God would give me strength to carry out what he had asked of me. I asked the Lord, "How long do you want me to fast?" I didn't get a response to that question, so I began to pool together resources on spiritual warfare, and obtained a journal to record what God would reveal to me during this time. On a daily basis, I found myself writing scriptures in my journal—scriptures on trust and confidence in God. I meditated on these words day and night.

On the eve of the coming New Year, my husband and I prayed, thanking God for what he had done and for his continued guidance throughout the coming year. No one other than God could have prepared us for what we were then faced with on January 1, 2007. There was an all-out attack on our finances. Bank accounts were frozen, credit card accounts...frozen. What did this mean? What was going on? I kept asking myself these questions. But the Holy Spirit gently reminded me of the storm. I managed to take hold of my breathless state, quickly centered myself, and began making calls to figure out the reason why all of this was happening. I systematically and calmly worked through the process—with my husband not so sure why and how I could be so at peace with this turn of events. After several weeks of phone calls and paperwork, we finally crossed that hurdle. Then, a month or so later, we were hit again. The next hurdle was a lawsuit. The accusations being brought against us were unbelievable. I knew we were in for a fight. I had no idea it would last five years, but God proved faithful. Throughout this five-year period, our finances were constantly threatened, our bank accounts frozen so many times. It became more like a glacier floating in the sea. We had lost the battle, but I knew that we had not lost the war!

We were slapped with a judgment of nearly two million dollars. Needless to say, that's enough to make anyone lose heart. But I kept the faith and stood on what God had spoken to me. You see, during my time of prayer and fasting, God had been preparing me—arming me with his Word and teaching me to stand on it no matter what may come my way. He was stretching and strengthening my

faith, teaching me a different level of endurance and patience.
One day, during the final days of my fasting, I was praying, and the Lord spoke to me: "It will be okay. I will take care of you." I answered, "Yes LORD." I had to stand on His promise that our situation would be okay. It wasn't always easy, but I constantly went back to the scriptures he had given me on trust and confidence. I meditated on them constantly. During this process, I encouraged others to trust God, not merely making cliché statements, but teaching others what I was experiencing…to trust Him. I truly learned the meaning of Philippians 4:7. *"And the peace of God, which passeth all understanding, shall keep your hearts and minds through Christ Jesus."* The peace that rested on me was amazing. I sometimes had to ask myself how I could be so at peace and so calm during such distressing events. It was all GOD!

As time marched on, the 2 million dollar judgment was overturned, but the war still wasn't over. The adversary was still kicking. We were then faced with a $300,000 judgment. I said, "God, you told me that this was going to be alright, and I trust you. You are a God that cannot lie and your Word will not return unto you void. Just continue to help me stand." And stand I did. Even when I didn't know how or understand why, I knew that I had to trust God and not man. I knew it didn't matter what it looked like…God was in control. I had to believe His report. I must admit that I sometimes grew weary and sometimes wanted to give up. There were times when I wanted to abandon my Christian duties, but the Holy Spirit would remind me of scriptures that I had studied. I often quoted Isaiah 50:7. *"The Lord will help me…I have not been humiliated, I will not be put to shame; therefore I have set my face like flint, and I know that I shall not be put to shame."* Galatians 6:9 was also a comfort to me. *"We must not get tired of doing good...we will reap at the proper time if we don't give up."* No matter how I felt physically, my beginning and end was God. After five long years, I had a conversation with my spouse and told him not to lose heart because God would take care of us as he always had—and no matter the outcome, he would never leave nor forsake us. He was disheartened, so I shared with him Jeremiah 29:11. *"For I know the plans I have for you, declare the LORD, plans to prosper you and not to harm you, plans to give you hope and a future."* I also shared with him that I truly believed we were on the verge of a breakthrough. Surely my feeling was correct.

And it truly was proven to be so! In the first month of 2012, in the midnight hour, we received a phone call that it was over. The ordeal was over! Plus, we received an apology to boot! Throughout this entire time, divine intervention was at work.

As many of you know, there are numbers that have a biblical meaning. The number 1, 5, and 12 are significant to my story. The number one represents unity, primacy, and independent of all other...the source of all others. So God is the one and only deity, the source of all, and all stand in need of Him. During my storm, God—and only God—was my source, my shield and buckler.

The spiritual significance of the number five is Grace...God's favor. Five is noteworthy, as it was five long years of legal proceedings that we had to endure; but it was, and is still, God's grace and favor that kept us throughout this trial. As mankind, I am weak; but with God, I am mighty because of His edifying grace.

Finally, the number twelve represents all that has to do with rule and perfection in government. Looking back, I can see God orchestrating his will on our behalf with those in position to make decisions concerning our lives. While things looked bleak in the natural realm, it was God's divine power setting things in order in the heavenly realm.

When God prompts you to do something, trust that he has already equipped you to weather the storm. It is a confident conviction you must have that God is bigger than your problems and circumstances. You must know, that you know, that you know...that God has the very last say-so. He is my closest confidant...the Great "I Am." Without Him, I can do nothing. You who are going through a storm...Be encouraged! Stay focused on God's Word! It is true! It is our weapon to fight the enemy! Don't put your confidence in the flesh, but on God; he is always with you. As Paul said, *"I press on toward the goal to win the prize for which God has called me heavenward in Christ Jesus."* To God be the glory!

LOVER

Carolyn Solomon

Long ago, I saw evidence of the one my soul craved. In my dreams, from the earliest of times, he came to me. But I could not recognize this entity I hungered for. Like a hazy apparition, without form, this being first emerged. That is when I felt his essence to be all-towering, all-consuming—a living unit that I desired and who loved me first.

This knowledge ignited within me a driving force, making me seek him constantly. Surprisingly, in night's sightless quiet, I seemed to discern him better; while during the light of day and life's occupying activity, he appeared elusive, absent, unfaithful and likely betraying me with some other.

As time went on, with little effort from me, the man persistently touched me and entered my life. He began to take form. I saw him in the awakening of spring when matting and blossoming begin. Summer's rebirth and lazy days announced his existence, but faintly. Fall's fading colors and announcement of change brought home, to some degree, his constant presence. Even winter's starkness, cold and severe, whispered proclamations of his tender care and sweet love for me.

But I required something more—real, concrete, a visible form, a name to help me know more about this entity…this being. Certainly, a physical, very present, real form was a requirement. I needed a solid shape or actual body—a body that consisted of mass or matter—someone like me.

Passing seasons proved not enough. Only a human body would do for me—made of flesh, bone and blood.

Then one day, I looked upon him. He came to me in the figure of a man called Adam. He appeared to me as a human figure, in the mold of a male: strong-limbed, ebony-hued, soft-spoken. Adam personified comeliness with his six-foot-four physique, adorned in a navy designer suit. The smart cut of Adam's jet-black wooly hair impressed, and love's sweet care that he lavished upon me fully enticed and won me over. All my wants and desires, emotional and physical, this mere man fulfilled. Adam supplied my every need. Nothing kept this man from supplying all I asked for. He gave freely and fully, so it seemed. He wooed me expertly and precisely, until I succumbed...yielding all...everything.

In matrimony, that blessed coupling, bonding state, I grew closer to Adam. I became as attracted to Adam as static persistently adheres to silk. And he, likewise, seemed to cleave to me. I dwelled in Utopia—that is, until time slipped past.

Days, weeks, months evolved into years and exposed life's frustrations, trails and sorrows. Man's fidelity is not constant. Man's loyalty is far from being consistent. Human nature is oftentimes painfully lacking and not always dependable. Human love is fragile and, too quickly, can fade. When love is new, man and woman can forget what they once had and seek satisfaction elsewhere. Vows are forgotten and thrown away...pushed aside. It is so easy to forget when seeking our own wants, needs and desires.

One particular incident in my life stands out. It treads in the waters of my mind, refusing to drown, or submerge and stay far below the surface. My life would have been easier if that occurrence would just die! That one incident was Adam's initial betrayal. It seems the first of anything always makes the strongest, most intense impression. Like a burn, it leaves a visible ugly wound or mark on the flesh. On our wedding day, Adam promised to love for better or worse and until death parted us. Learning of his betrayal from others scattered my world into a trillion pieces. Why didn't he tell me?

My life became a hell. I existed like a lost soul drowning in my misery and anger. Believing revenge would give me satisfaction…pay Adam back…make him feel what I felt, I proceeded to commit the same offense that Adam was guilty of. I betrayed him. The biggest mistake of my life had occurred. After that act of betrayal, I dwelled in an even deeper hell. A worse misery beset me. I found no solace. My life wavered out of balance and I felt lost and separated…disjointed from the whole. My soul lingered in limbo, in a state devoid of hope. Life had little meaning. All joy had vanished from my world.

In spite of this pain and anger and despair, I survived and life went on. After a tremendous struggle, and what felt like constant prayer, I somehow forgave and somehow healed. In that process of hurting, healing and forgiving, I found a treasure—a priceless jewel. By putting aside the trivial temporary things of this world, thinking only of myself, lusting after material possessions and physical pleasures, I found something far better and a trillion times more precious. Revenge is not for me to execute, but for the Lord to perform. I can now put my wonderful husband Adam in the right perspective. I count him as only a small part of the whole that I thirst for. Material treasures of this world and my dear Adam, a mere man, I now know will never completely fulfill my needs. Temporal, fleeting things can never fill the longing in my heart. My soul yearns for more—so much more. I now live securely--knowing there is One who loves me with a perfect, everlasting love. He will never betray me—never forsake me—never leave me.

Yes, the veil has fallen from my eyes and from my soul. I can now see clearly. This blessing has enabled my Adam and me to forgive one another—and we recently celebrated 50 years of marriage! I am also grateful that creation has revealed the root of all existence. Spring's rebirth, honey-dripping days of summer, autumn's yield and winter's cold still does proclaim the all-encompassing, very real presence I sought so long ago. Adam's splendid physical appearance, the fine cut of his clothing and hair still bring smiles of delight to my eyes and heart. But I now realize that the things of this world are temporary—and Adam, me, and all of us in the physical form are destined for more. I rest assured that the Creator, who gives life to all, is the Alpha and Omega, the beginning and the end.

This knowledge enriches me—making life better and my burden lighter. To declare that my existence is now perfect—always blissful and smooth-sailing—would not be truthful. In all honesty, I can declare that I do know who wooed and loved me first—before anyone else. He knew me even before I was conceived or thought of. He is the root, the core of my life—all life—and the Entity that my whole being yearns for. He is the foundation of all creation. He goes by many names. Some call him Counselor, Consoler, Yahweh and Jehovah. I see Him in countless configurations. The universe proclaims His glorious expanse. Earth heralds His greatness. His majesty shines forth even in my dear, imperfect, very human Adam—and in me—and in every human being. None can compare to the Creator. He, the wooer of all, loved me first. He gave his only Son up to die for me. For this I give Him praise for my life! I shout to the whole world: "God is the Consummate Lover!"

SUICIDE IS NOT AN OPTION (A Testimony of Survival)

Faith Larkins

I think I have always known there was a God, even when I did not have a relationship with Him. Somehow, for some reason, He was always there for me. I was born in Detroit, Michigan, and raised by my mother and father. I am the youngest of four girls.

When I think back on my family and the years of my youth, I see a dysfunctional unit. My father was a strict disciplinarian who had difficulty demonstrating his love to his daughters, and oftentimes to his wife. My mother over-compensated to her daughters the love they did not feel from their father. At various times in our lives, each of my sisters and I would "act out" as a result of our upbringing.

As a young child, I was generally happy most of the time. But at other times, I was disturbed by what appeared to be the disintegration of my family. My father was a hard-working man, but was also an alcoholic and abuser. The abuse towards his children did not come in the form of beatings, but rather from his inability to demonstrate his love for us. On the other hand, his abuse toward my mother took a more "hands on" approach.

I recall several times when my father would slap my mother, but one particular incident stands out in my mind. My sisters and I were sleeping in our bunk beds in our bedroom when my father came home late one night. I heard my parents arguing and I assumed my mother must have waited up for him. As I peeked from our bedroom door, I saw my father pulling my mother by her ankle from the couch she was sitting on. I do not remember if he struck her, but I only remember racing into the living room to protect my mother. When I reached the living room, my father had his forearm around my mother's neck and a handgun pressed against her temple! Frantic, my sisters and I screamed for him to let her go. His words were unintelligible to me, but I could see the fear in my mother's eyes. God's grace intervened and my father accidentally dropped the gun. I quickly grabbed it and my eldest sister took it from me and threw it in the basement. Fearing for our lives, my mother, sisters and I ran from our house to a neighbor's home. The next morning we re-entered our home and found our father passed out on the couch with a shotgun resting by his hand.

As you might guess, this left an indelible impression on my young fragile mind. It changed how I viewed my father, and for many years I hated him for what he had done. I was also not too fond of my mother during these years because she stayed with my father out of obligation. They would work through their problems and my father would begin to drink less—but I was changed from that point on. I later discovered that my paternal grandfather was an alcoholic who abused his wife to the point that she jumped from a window and to her death. My father had been there.

As I grew up, religion was barely introduced to me by my family. We were "holiday" church-goers. I found this unusual, as my mother's mother was a preacher. But in any event, I had discovered a desire to know more about God than my parents could or would teach me.

My best friend was on fire for God and her family attended church services regularly. I was pleased when she invited me to go with them. I began attending Unity Baptist Church with her and her family when I was approximately twelve years old. I found that I loved the church environment as much as I loved her and her family. I soon became a member of Unity Baptist Church and a constant visitor at my best friend's home. It seemed as if I were baptized into the church family and into my best friend's family as well. I spent a great deal of time with her and her family, often favoring her family over my own.

Throughout most of my teenage years, I stayed true to God. However, when I enrolled and was accepted at Western Michigan University in 1983, my relationship with God began to deteriorate. As a child I had been somewhat sheltered and had very few life experiences; so when I went away to college—away from my parents, I felt free. College life exposed me to many things—and not all of them were good.

The first year of college went well. My grade point average (GPA) was good. As I began to meet people and became familiar with my surroundings, I began to attend a variety of functions. The more functions (parties) I attended, the more I was exposed to. I drank (alcohol) prior to attending college, but being away at college merely increased that behavior. Alcohol was not the only vice I would incur, but I established an occasional use of narcotics as well.

The parties, drinking and the riotous lifestyle would have its effects on me as well as on my grades. After my sophomore year, my GPA was a disturbing 1.89. My parents, who were paying for my college education, were not pleased, so I began to take a more active role in paying for my higher education.

I am not proud of my college years. I recognize now I was depraved and reckless. Every action, every situation, had a result. Looking back on that time in my life, I see where my life changed. I was headed down a path of great loneliness and deep depression. The happy child that I had been was gone. My self-esteem declined. I consumed large amounts of alcohol to drown my sorrows. I became very isolated. Now, I know that this was exactly what the enemy wanted.

This isolation caused by deep depression shut me off from the outside world. It was further compounded by my alcohol use. I spent my nights alone, drinking and feeling sorry for myself; and my days were spent in the classroom. As this cycle continued, soon thoughts of suicide entered my mind and I often thought of dying. When those thoughts came, I would reach out to one of my sisters to "talk" me through it.

In 1987, as I prepared to graduate from college, my thoughts were never far from death. I simply could not imagine my life staying the way it was. I did not want to live the way I was living. Still, I felt powerless to make any changes on my own. I began to sink deeper into sadness, deeper into depression, and my thoughts circled around suicide…or rather, how to commit suicide. Should I cut my wrists or take some pills? Should I get a gun? Even as I asked these questions, it seemed that the angel of the Lord would ask me, "What about your family? How would it affect them? Who will take care of your cat?" As I pondered each set of questions, I would hear the Holy Spirit urging me toward life and living. I would hear God encouraging me…telling me to call my sister. And each time, that's what I would do.

My sister was very gracious—talking to me, crying with me, encouraging me. And at the end of our conversations, she would make me promise to call her the next morning; and wanting to be true to my word, I always did so. Still, I was far from being out of the woods. My battles were fierce—consistent and ever increasing.

After college in 1989, I began a career in law enforcement in Lansing, Michigan. As a newly hired employee, I was enthusiastic about my employment, but my excitement would wane and give rise to disgruntlement. I discovered that good employment was not the answer to bad living. My careless lifestyle took on a new life, and now it was not my grades that suffered, but my employment. It seemed I was trapped in a vicious cycle from which I could not escape. Each failed attempt pushed me deeper into the mire that was my existence. Where was God?

In 1990-1991, a friend attempted to re-introduce me to God; but angry at the state of my life and with Him, I would hear none of it. I dismissed her, cursed at her and threatened her each time she would mention God. After all, wasn't God the reason I was in this situation? Where was He when I needed Him? Why would He allow me to go through these things? I wanted nothing to do with Him. I had tried Him in the past and my life was no better as a result. I became increasingly angry.

But my friend never gave up trying to evangelize me. And finally, her persistence paid off and simply wore me into submission. During this time, my return to Christ was from no real effort of mine, but rather due to the fervent, persistent prayer of a righteous soul. In 1992-1993, I attended New Jerusalem Church regularly. I was around 26 years old when I was baptized a second time. I slowly began to see some changes in myself and even began to see God move in my life. I gained a foundation in God on which His Son could build. I did not know it then, but I would later understand that this was the very foundation that would one day save my life.

For a time, life was good. I was reasonably happy and had a decent life; but it was not long before the enemy reared his ugly head and the battle began again.

In every aspect of my life—personal and professional, the enemy began to attack me. I regularly experienced stressful situations that resulted in blinding migraines and bouts of alopecia (hair loss). I was often irritable and argumentative. Once again, I hated my life and was desperate for change. I self-medicated with alcohol and cigarettes. I wanted to be oblivious to the world outside—and for the most part, I was just that.

I often struggled to find the reason why I found myself in these situations. My search for love was certainly part of the reason. As a child, I had been deprived and desperately wanted to feel love from my father. As a child, I was often disappointed—over and over. But since my father never received from his father, he really did not know how to demonstrate love to his own children. My mother nurtured us to the point of suffocation, but it was the rejection I felt from my father and my subsequent search for that illusive love that would lay a path for destruction in my life.

Being loved was so very important to me that I looked elsewhere to find my father's love. But no one person held that love for me. I would find that only my Heavenly Father can provide this love. I continued to trudge through my life, and brought with me the baggage of rejection, isolation and depression. I identified with the scripture in Matthew 12:43-45 which speaks of an unclean spirit being swept from a man but with nothing to fill the space, the spirit returns to its home and brings seven more spirits with it. This seemed so true in my case.

In 1995, I moved from Lansing back to Detroit. I settled into a new employment position and made my way through life one day at a time. I pushed back those feelings of depression and tried to live a normal life. I settled into my sister's home and began to search the area for another church home. For months, I search every Sunday, but it would be another eight years before I found the right church. During this time—as has been the pattern anytime there is a lull in my spiritual growth, I returned to what had been comfortable for me, the world. But this time, the difference was that the Father impressed upon me to read the Bible, Genesis through Revelation. I believe that, during these times of study, Jesus Christ was shaping and building inside me. I believe He was preparing and strengthening me for the days to come.

During the eight years that I wandered the world, Jesus was never far from my thoughts. Even though I was neither happy nor sad, I was surviving. I knew it was important to find a church home. I had to find my covering. I remember once telling someone that I felt death was chasing me. I knew if I continued down the path I was on, death would surely catch up to me and overtake me.

I again felt myself in a downward spiral—and I once again found comfort in alcohol. I often believed there was something desperately wrong with me and that I was gradually losing my mind. As the struggles of my life continued, depression re-surfaced one last, potentially disastrous, time.

What brought about the depression, I do not exactly recall. I only remember feeling as if my life was spiraling out of control. Living in my own home, I got drunk and decided I had had enough and was not going to live like this any longer. I recall grabbing my gun and sitting on the edge of my bed…contemplating death. I was so very sad and so very tired. I remember just wanting all the pain to end. As I sat there, I could hear the enemy goading me towards death. "Just do it," he said. "Your life is not getting any better." As the kingdom of darkness beckoned me, I could hear another voice—what I believed to be my angel—saying, "Call your sister. Call Lori." I considered the lateness of the hour, but I continued to hear the words time after time: "Call Lori." As I dialed my sister's phone number, I prayed she would answer…and she did! As my thoughts spilled out to her and I told her my dilemma, she spoke kindly and softly. Her words, filled with love (and, I'm sure, a bit of terror), soothed and reassured me. At the end of the call, she insisted that I put the gun away, then go to bed; and, as usual, she made me promise to call her when I awoke the next morning. I promised.

Before I went to sleep that night, I cried out to God. I told Him I could no longer live a life without hope. I told Him that He had to do something so that I would not find myself at this place again. I made a promise to God that night—that if He brought me through this, I would never again consider suicide as an option for my life.

The morning came, and I called my sister as I had promised. We talked a bit more and she advised me that I should seek professional help. I felt I had nothing to lose and possibly my sanity to gain. I got a referral from my doctor and visited a psychiatrist. I had several meetings with this doctor, and each time I met with her, she asked me why I was really there. After the fourth meeting, she pressed the question even further—Why was I there? I told her something was wrong with me. She was adamant that there was nothing wrong with me. I left her office feeling very confused. Surely she was mistaken.

I was on the verge of desperation until I walked into the receptionist's office. There in front of me, on a bulletin board, was a flyer that told me about a local church that was minutes from my home. I inquired about it and learned that it was just the type of place I had been looking for. Finally, weeks later, I decided to attend my first service. Several weeks later, in June 2004, I joined Living Bread Ministries, West Gate Church and rededicated my life to Jesus Christ. I still have struggles but now I am so much better equipped to handle them. God, in all His omnipotence, has provided a way for me to escape every difficult situation.

Thinking back on all those years gone by, I am amazed at God's saving grace and His mercy—and I am forever drawn by His love. Not once did He allow me to slip from His hand of protection. Some injuries were self-inflicted while others were not; but in either case, He was faithful to cover me, to heal me and to stand me up each time I fell. My Lord has never left me nor forsaken me and I am so grateful for that. He has loved me as no other man could. He has kept His promises to me and I have kept my promise to Him. Because of Him, I have never longed for the escape of death again and I can gladly say that suicide is not, nor will ever be again, an option for my life! Amen.

FAITH RENEWED

Amy J. Meyer-Johnson

I sat and reflected on that hot, summer night—going over so many details in my head about the course my life had taken over the past fifteen years. I sipped my iced tea and thought about decisions I had made, both good and bad (but mostly bad), and how my life at that time might have been different had I made alternate choices. What's done was done though. With one bad marriage under my belt and a second one in shambles, I couldn't help but hope for better things to come. I had lined up a great new job at a university. The job seemed destined to be mine. The entire hiring process ran so smoothly and everything fell into place quickly.

I had five healthy children who were my heart and my life. My two oldest daughters were hundreds of miles away from me for long periods of time due to the decision of a prejudiced divorce attorney and judge. The three that I was raising full time, two sons and a daughter had all been diagnosed with Attention Deficit/Hyperactivity Disorder (ADD/ADHD). But the whole bunch of them meant everything to me.

My current marriage was bad—even worse than the first had been. My husband had a drug addiction and had been unfaithful—involved in multiple extra-marital affairs. As much as I hate to admit it, he was a wolf in sheep's clothing and quite the charmer. But I was trying to think positively. Maybe this new job would be a turning point. After all, the pay was $4.00 more per hour than I had been making over the past few years, I had full benefits, paid holidays and vacations, and when the time came, I could send the kids to college tuition free! Something good had to come from this.

I got the new job, and a couple of weeks into it, I was really pleased and was gaining some needed self-esteem. But something else was also happening. I felt that something was strange—not right physically—just not like myself. I first passed it off as simply stress—I had a new routine and the kids were beginning a new school year. Another week went by and it suddenly occurred to me what that "strange" feeling could be. I had all the signs of being pregnant. But I couldn't be! My husband and I weren't getting along, he was living away from home with another woman, and we barely saw one another. Even though I told myself it was impossible, I had to face the truth that baby number six was on the way.

I was afraid. My husband had lost his teaching job earlier that year. I was paying child support for my two girls who lived apart from me much of the time due to custody issues and a messy divorce, and I was solely supporting the other three. By the time a new baby arrived, I would have been working at my new job for only eight months. I knew that I would have needed to be there at least twelve months to be granted a paid maternity leave—and I was already 40 years old! What would I do? I did the only thing I could do—pray. I began to talk to God the way I always had, as if He were my earthly father right there beside me, because I knew He was truly present. I talked to God, I cried, I asked questions and I apologized for my faith being weak and for having any doubt that He could help me through this. "Why? Why now? You know my husband is without a job, that he's unfaithful and doesn't help with the kids that are already here. Why, Lord? I know your word says that You won't give me more than I can bear, but I really don't understand any of this."

I tossed and turned all night. I knew I had to tell my boss. I didn't want him to think I had been keeping this from him or had concealed my pregnancy to land the job. I knew there was no sense in putting off the inevitable. I would just go ahead and do it. The next morning I knocked on his office door and asked my boss I could have a few minutes of his time. "Sure Amy. Come in and sit down," he said. I took a deep breath and said, "I'll get right to the point. I really love this job and I hope to be here for many years to come. However, I discovered during the past week that I'm expecting another child. I'm aware that I won't have enough time in to take maternity leave by the time I deliver, but I'm willing to put the baby in full time daycare at four weeks of age. I understand completely if you want to look for someone else to fill my position but I'd be ever so grateful if you'd consider keeping me on under the conditions I just mentioned." Wow! I managed to tell him without falling apart. He breathed a heavy sigh and looked somewhat disappointed. He silently contemplated his response for what seemed like forever, but it was probably only a few seconds. "Amy, I like you. You seem to fit well into our team here nicely. Only four weeks off you say?" "Yes, Sir. I promise," I said. He nodded and said, "I think that can be worked out." I can't express how relieved I was to hear those words! It was going to break my heart to put the baby in daycare at four weeks old—but I had to do it.

Autumn was beginning—my favorite season. I loved everything about it—the colors, the smells, the anticipation of holidays to come. But this year was different. I was a little less joyful and a lot more anxious than usual. I still had so many unanswered questions. How will I support yet another child alone…on an income that is already stretched as badly as the waistband on my husband's BVDs, I thought, as I placed them in his dresser. Why do I still do it? Why do I still set out a plate for him at every meal, hoping that he'll walk through the door and join us? His affairs were numerous and so painful for me. And even worse than the affairs he had with women was the one he was having with crack cocaine and heroin!

Thanksgiving came and went and it was time to begin preparing for Christmas. It was during that time of preparation—that Advent season—that I began to receive my answers from God.

One night before I went to sleep, I had yet another long conversation with God. "Father, I still don't understand how I'm going to do this. I know that you have entrusted me to raise this child that I'm carrying to love and serve you—but how, Lord?" I closed my eyes and opened my Bible. The pages fell open to the story of the coming of Jesus in the Book of Matthew. As I read the scripture, God answered my questions. If the woman He chose to carry His only begotten Son could endure a long, difficult journey, labor on a donkey, childbirth in a filthy barn with no professional medical staff, why was I questioning that God could see me through this? I was ashamed of my fear and my lack of faith. I slept well that night—and had the blessed assurance that, with God, all things are truly possible.

Another Wisconsin winter did its best to wear me down. There had been almost one hundred feet of snow, and my old van had seen better days and started only when it wanted to. At times, the kids and I were waking at 4 a.m. so that we would have enough time to catch the city bus to school and work. The looks I got from people staring at my

ever growing mid-section as I was trudging through the snow with an already large family were disheartening.
But spring was on its way. My baby was due in the third week of April—Easter week that year. I had been using my accumulated lunch hours to go to my pre-natal appointments. I saved all of my "sick days" to be used during the four weeks that I was allowed off from work following his birth. He would even things out—three girls and three boys. The week before my new bundle was born, my boss called me into his office. He handed me an envelope and asked me to open it. In it I found a check equal to two weeks of my pay; and I had enough paid leave saved up to cover the other two weeks I would be away from work. "Thank you!" I said, as I tried not to cry. Those simple words didn't seem sufficient, but they were all I had to offer.

It was Good Friday and the kids and I were just returning home from church in the afternoon. As I pulled into the driveway, I noticed more than the usual number of cars parked in front of our apartment building. Three friends of mine were unloading what seemed to be an endless stream of bags and boxes onto the sidewalk. One of them called to my sons, who were 11 and 10 at the time, to come and help bring it all inside. My youngest daughter, only 5 years old, got in on the act as well. There were bags and bags of new and gently used clothes for the baby. There were enough bags of disposable diapers in every imaginable size to make ten neat rows across my bedroom wall—and they each stood about four feet high!

I was overwhelmed yet again. God had used the people in my life to literally pour out a blessing to me that I scarcely had room to contain!

Later that night, the doorbell rang. There stood a woman from work, whom I had met only once before, about a month or so earlier, at a retreat we both attended. She asked me to walk outside with her to her truck. In the back of the truck was a beautiful wooden crib, all sorts of bedding, an infant bathtub, towels and even more baby clothing. "I was thinking maybe you could use this stuff." she said. "I only have one son who is now five and my husband and I divorced last year. I won't need these items any longer. If you don't mind these 'used' things, you're welcome to have them." I could hardly believe it! She had just pulled up to my house and provided me with the only items I still needed in preparation for my baby to be born. I thanked her over and over again as she and I and the kids brought it all inside.

That night, as I laid there in bed rubbing my abdomen to soothe my youngest son's kicking, I began to talk with God as I did every night. "Lord, please forgive me for ever doubting you. Thank you for placing the perfect people in my life at exactly the right moment. Thank you for the safe delivery of this healthy, beautiful baby boy. I know that it's all taken care of and in your capable hands."

At 5:37 a.m., on the Thursday after Easter, my sixth child and third son came into this world. He continues to bring me so much joy. Through this child, God has shown me that what looks to be impossible is possible by trusting in Him.

ONCE I KNEW, THEN CAME MY BREAKTHROUGH

Linda Jo White

Like most of us, I have faced many challenges in my life. And like many of us, a few of those challenges plagued me for years and years. For most of my life, these challenges had me thinking that I would never amount to anything—that I wasn't worthy of good things—that I had always been, and would always be, a failure.

Disgusting... Ruined... Shameful... Disgraceful... Ugly... Worthless... Useless... Invalid... Defeated...
I was convinced that I would end up dying young—without hope—and in a messed up, jacked up situation. I didn't feel worthy of anything good; and, therefore, didn't think I would ever have anything good.

This year, on the 28th of May, I will be 47 years old—and from the time I was 19 until I was 39, I had struggled with one particular Set Point of Limitations. For 20 years, this particular challenge plagued me...20 years. Now, looking back, it had been a turning point in my life that was meant to take me out and destroy me forever. I was attacked by those things that come to steal, kill and destroy. And for 20 years, this Set Point did just that—stole my peace and joy—killed my dreams and hopes—destroyed the vision of those things that I was predestined to become.

Does this sound like something you are going through? Then I implore you to keep reading. I beg you to keep reading; because, like me, you too can break through! I hope that by the time you finish reading my story, you will have a tool that will help you obtain your breakthrough—because I truly believe that, if it's possible for me, it's possible for you. I believe you were created for a unique purpose. I believe that your purpose is part of the answer to the questions of your generation. You are not living only by chance…a fluke…or a mistake. Rather, the Creator of the Universe, God himself, formed you with a specific task in mind. This I know.

You may ask me, "Well, how do you know these things?" And I will tell you, "Because I know, that I know, that I know—and I know…that I know…that I know because of what I learned that enabled me to break through!

One favorite scripture I've come to know is Hosea 4:6: "My people are destroyed for lack of knowledge." That's how it is worded in the King James Version. But I like the way this passage of scripture reads in the New Living Testament: "My people are being destroyed because they don't know me." I want to define the word "destroy" for you, because this is deep and I want you to see the depth of the effects that Set Points have on our lives.

The definition of "destroy" is: "To reduce to useless fragments, a useless form, or remains, as by rending, burning, or dissolving; injure beyond repair or renewal; demolish; ruin; annihilate. To put an end to; extinguish. To kill; slay. To render ineffective or useless; nullify; neutralize; invalidate. To defeat completely." And the definition of the word "know" is: "To perceive or understand as fact or truth; to apprehend clearly and with certainty."

Here's what I did with those two definitions—and it helped me tremendously: When I took the definitions of those two words and plugged them into Hosea 4:6, I found that it read something like this: "My people are reduced to useless fragments, useless forms and remains, are injured beyond repair or renewal; demolished; ruined; annihilated; put an end to; extinguished; killed; slayed; rendered ineffective and useless; nullified; neutralized; invalidated and defeated completely because they have a lack of perception, understanding of my facts and truths and cannot apprehend clearly or with certainty, my truths." Now that's really deep, isn't it?

For 20 years, from the time I was 19 until I was 39, my life was an example of the above scripture—because of what happened to me at 19 years old. It was devastating and it destroyed me for 20 years. But I thank God for His grace, His mercy, and His promise—that all things work for my good as I truly love the Lord and have been called and created for a purpose.

Here's what happened. When I was 19 years old, I was gang-raped. It was a Saturday night after a semi-professional hockey game. I was with some folks whom I thought were my friends. I ended up at a place with more people I thought were my friends and some people that I did not know at all—but I thought it was a "safe" place. How did I end up there? Earlier that evening, I had felt sorry for another person who didn't have a ride home after the hockey game, and I had given her a ride to my friend's house. Once I was there, I stayed for quite a while, then realized it was probably too late to make the 45-minute drive home. I gave in to my friend's invitation to stay at her place and go home in the morning. So I said goodnight to the few remaining guests and went to sleep in the guest bedroom.

Then it happened—the Set Point of Limitations that was designed to steal, kill and destroy the rest of my life. I was abruptly awakened about 4 a.m. by three semi-professional hockey players who had taken it upon themselves, and with the urging of my friend, to enter the guest room and begin taking turns having sex with me. Here I was, still fully clothed…with my skirt hiked up…being violated in a most intimate way. I had given none of them permission to violate me, and when I had gone to bed that night, I had no idea what was in store for me. The three of them laughed, took turns raping me repeatedly, spoke nasty and terrible words to me that I had never heard before. They mocked me…made jokes about me. It was simply surreal. When they were done, I was left in the dark with only a little light from the living room shining in through the crack of the door. I heard them rustle around for a quick minute then leave the house. Then I heard nothing. I don't remember what time I left; but I just remember feeling so ashamed—straightening my skirt and walking out of the guest room, only to discover that I was alone. There was no one home—not even my friend—and so I left.

Later that afternoon, I received a phone call from this so-called "friend" who asked me "how it was." It was then that I realized she had set me up. I didn't realize that apparently, this was an activity that my "friend" and others in this social circle had come to enjoy regularly. In her eyes, she assumed that every girl coveted the opportunity to "make it" with a semi-pro hockey player. I learned that I was not the only one who had been set up like this; and because "others were doing it," she felt it would be okay to set me up. And so, she felt justified in her motivation for giving the three young, aspiring, clean-cut athletes permission to rape me!

Another favorite scripture I've come to know is found in Luke 23:24—and it is the words spoken by Jesus as He was dying on the cross, as the folk around Him are casting lots for His clothes. Jesus said, "Father, forgive them, for they know not what they do." I did not come to know the reality of this truth until I was 34 years old. It was then that, upon understanding clearly and apprehending this certain truth, I finally forgave my friend—and the three men, who had been used as vessels to try to steal, kill and destroy me. It had been fifteen years that I had been carrying around this baggage and bondage—dealing with the junk and nastiness of that day—way back to when I was just 19 years old. More importantly, I came to forgive myself—and I felt a "loosening."

Five years later, on November 19th, 2004, I received my breakthrough—and yes, I remember the date, the time, and even the weather and smells in the air that weekend. Over the course of those five years, I had come to a place where the Set Points slowly "loosened"—a little bit here—a little bit there. And more knowledge led to more loosening. The more I learned, the more I began to realize and know things. The more I began to know, the less I was destroyed. I came to know that "God is" and that "He is a Rewarder of those who diligently seek Him." He would never leave or forsake me and all things would work for my good because He promised me so in His Word. And because He was God, and not a man that He should lie, I could count on what He said about me and my circumstances to be true. I was growing stronger and beginning to dream again. I had come to know hope—and I could begin to see a light at the end of the tunnel. I knew that one day…one day…I was going to be free.

And then it happened—the breakthrough!
It was on November 19th, 2004, at a little church in Detroit, Michigan, at a Women's Encounter Weekend. As I sat in one of the sessions, I came to know the following: Psalm 139:14 says, "I will praise thee; for I am fearfully and wonderfully made." (KJV) Me!!! Fearfully and wonderfully made!!! The Psalm goes on to say, in the New Living Translation, that God's workmanship…me...was marvelous! The last of the chains finally broke…I was free! I finally had the knowledge that I had been created by the Creator of the Universe—and I am a miracle! I am a miraculous, remarkable phenomenon that was formed with His hands…for a purpose! Suddenly, all the limitations were gone. I can now overcome the impossible with faith in a God of all possibilities. I can do all things through Christ who will always strengthen me.
I am chosen and I am victorious.
I was created with marvelous gifts and talents.
I can use those gifts just as God has planned.
I can be courageous and press forward with confidence.
I know that God will never leave or forsake me.
I will no longer suffer from lack of knowledge.
I will seek out wisdom and knowledge.
I can have great peace in my life.

And so, I leave you today with this encouraging knowledge: You are just as special as I am in God's eyes. Everything He has promised to me, He has promised to you. Everything available to me is available to you—and, like me, you were chosen and created for a specific purpose.

God loves you so very much. He will strengthen you and uphold you and give you peace as you come to know and seek Him. He is no respecter of persons. What He's done for one, He'll do for another. He promises us that, if we "seek first His Kingdom and His Righteousness, all things will be added unto us." But you've got to know this for yourself! Like me, you've got to know…that you know…that you know.

So as I have been made free and am on the path to fulfilling the purpose for which I was created, I would like to leave you with this statement that I have come to tell many people whose paths I've crossed: It's true that I know more than some and not as much as others; but what I know, I know. And because I know, no one can take it from me—and I will never suffer again!

This is my prayer and hope for you today: Know…that you know…that you know…and you too will have your breakthrough!

KICKED OUT OF PARADISE, RESTORED IN GOD'S PROMISES

Judith S. Cooper

As we moved toward our 10th wedding anniversary, God showed me in a dream a desert without footprints, and I was walking eastward on the hot sands with a few faithful friends from our ministry. In the stretch of the distance, I faintly saw the image of three large camels and three statues resembling physical bodies standing in a postured position waiting for my arrival. As I drew closer, it appeared that the camels, lying comfortably, were draped with expensive apparel over their faces; and in between their massive humps were tapestry, beautiful linen, water canteens and silk pillows. I drew nearer to them, and after a closer view of their stature and image of strength, I was impressed that these camels had been assigned to me to ensure that my children were comfortable for what seemed would be a very long journey. The statue-like bodies were men dressed in Moroccan style clothing. In my dream, they eventually assisted my friends by saddling up my two sons and one daughter, ages 10, 7 and 5, on their respective camels. One of the men then handed me three long thick leather straps to gauge the direction as I walked westward with my children, following footsteps that now appeared and would show me the way in my wilderness experience.

In the days to come, I thought about the dream until it left my spiritual meditation. During this time, I had the unction to speak with my sister requesting to spend time with her one weekend at her new house. I would have never imagined that I was headed for a turn of events that would cause an emotional, traumatic change in my life.

On October 14, 1996—out of nowhere—completely and unexpectedly—the understanding and interpretation of my dream brought on an act of utter disbelief. That day, coming home from my evening class, my ex-husband and father of our three children met me at the door He asked that I come in and sit down so that we could talk together. He told me, "God said, you are to no longer be my wife." I looked at him in disbelief, shocked and stunned, and told him, "God didn't tell you that! Whatever it is, we can make this work! God doesn't like divorce!" I cried out. But my voice of concern didn't matter. His own decision and discussion concerning our marriage was short-lived in his mind. I could see that nothing I said no longer mattered to him. He told me to leave the house immediately, and he recommended that I go and stay with my sister. I went toward the side door from the breezeway to enter the house and talk with my children; but he told me it would be best that I not see our children, and instructed me to just leave the house.

The door closed behind me. I felt the coldness in the atmosphere. A cold chill swept across my face, down to my hands, down my back. There was a strange quietness and stillness in the air as I looked up at the dark blue sky. I felt God's anger as I fixed my eyes on the heavens. I sought the Lord for His direction. Thoughts were swirling in my head, but still I focused on the well-being of my children. What would they think? How would they feel with their mother not there for them every morning? I felt myself falling apart emotionally. I wanted to react. I wanted to retaliate toward my children's father, but a voice in my inner spirit said, "You have to be strong! Your children will need you! Move forward!" "Yes, Lord," I thought. "I have to move now!" It was near midnight and I needed to find shelter. I recalled a conversation with my sister about a month ago and headed to the other side of the city to pay her an unexpected visit. I didn't recall the drive to her house, only the knock on her door and her welcomed embrace.

I was kicked out of Paradise. I was tossed out into a world of obscurity—no longer shielded, protected or secure. I was on my own. The life I had lived as a faithful pastor's wife, a devoted and caring mother, and an intercessor cultivating many spiritual relationships within our ministry—all this was no longer within reach. This had all been orchestrated by one man's decision. Early in my Christian walk, I had learned that God was a God of decency and of order; and in conjunction with that, God's design on marriages is specifically for intimate engagement of a supportive partnership and spiritual unity between a man and a woman. I had never heard of God suddenly writing off a marriage for no cause. There were vows and commitments to consider in our marriage. As I thought about the Paradise I once knew, I identified a familiar spirit that had invaded the essence of my sacred place. It had colored itself with truth and honesty toward me; and with spiritual perception, I later discovered that it was the single factor of deception and lies with my "garden." It was apparent that Adam had bitten into an apple given to him by a temptress; and the seductive effects were irreparable.

Based on man's decision, I had to set holy precedence and order in my life. I believe God was giving me a new page of history to share my trials and tribulations. I was eager to find myself and to be true to myself and others God put in my path. It was tough functioning through the deep-rooted bitterness and anger I had toward my children's father. This was a battleground I had to overcome. The enemy wanted to take hold of my mind, to hold it hostage and chain me into dark depression; but I refused to allow the enemy to win. No matter how I felt, I was not giving up on my relationship with God. I forced myself to pray and to remain in a state of prayer. I received God's chastisement in my secret place and willed Him to process it through me. I remained true to my calling, my obligation as a mother, and my proper role. I exercised. I taught my children to love God with all their heart and their soul…and to respect their parents. I remained celibate. More importantly, with the strength of God's hand on my life, my plan and determination was to rebuild my life over…brick by brick…on a sure foundation.

One morning, I realized I had reached the height of my restoration in God's promises. What seemed to be an eternity of misery was over and done in the blink of an eye. I woke up to freedom! What an amazing feeling! I shouted and praised God for healing me as I lay on my sofa bed. I was no longer oppressed. I was free in my mind…free in my spirit…full of love, hope and joy. My day felt different and new…it looked different…it was different. The blinds were open and they looked good…welcoming in my new path. Years of suffering with blame and shame were now gone. I was finally free…restored. I have been sketched and drafted to be an original submission of God's finished work. My wilderness experience led me to uncover my spiritual identity and freedom…as a unique woman with a voice…to break through any stumbling block that attempts to stand in my way!

SOME DREAMS TELL LIES

Apostle Londen Winters

My mother and father never married, and my stepfather and mother separated when I was eleven years old. About a year later, my mother began seeing a man that I didn't like. Being in his presence made me feel sick to my stomach and I stayed as far away from him as I could. I didn't know why I didn't like him, but I could plainly see that he liked me by the things he said to me and the way he watched me when my mother wasn't around. Within four months, he had moved in with us. That's when my life began to change.

On three different occasions, while my mother was asleep, he tiptoed into the bedroom where my sister and I slept. He covered my mouth with his left hand and whispered for me to be quiet; then began fondling my body. Once he finished what he wanted to do, he would kiss my lips lightly and tiptoe out of our bedroom. I couldn't believe this was happening to me! I was terrified! Each time, I would cry quietly during the ordeal, and when he left, I would cover my head with my pillow and cry out loud. This terrible time in my life began to affect me to the point that I could barely sleep and night—because I never knew when, or if, he was going to come back into our room. My speech was affected; I started stuttering when I spoke. I couldn't concentrate on my schoolwork; and when class ended, I would get very nervous because I didn't know what to expect when I got home. All I could do was wonder how my mother's boyfriend could do such a thing to me? I loved my mother so much. How was I going to tell her about it?

My mother and I had a very close relationship and I just knew that, when I would tell her what happened, this horror in my life would come to an end. I thought wrong.

After the third time I was attacked, I got enough nerve to write my mother a letter that told what her boyfriend had done. I put the letter in her main dresser drawer. When I arrived home from school, before I entered the front door, she called out my name and told me to come to her bedroom. I was so excited and thought to myself, "She's going to hold me in her arms and tell me that she's sorry about what happened." Instead, she held the letter close to my face, looked deeply into my hurt-filled eyes and said: "As long as you live, you better not ever write me a letter like this again." She tore the letter in half.

I was horrified! I froze for a moment, staring at her in disbelief with tears running down my face. I couldn't believe what I had heard. I waited for another response, thinking that she would rephrase what she had said and hold me and tell me she was sorry about what her boyfriend had done—but the words never came from her mouth.

Three months later, she broke up with her boyfriend. When he moved out, our relationship changed tremendously. My mother didn't talk to me as much as she had in the past. She became very "stand-offish." Why had she changed towards me? She had raised me to always tell the truth—and I had done just that! But in spite of how she treated me, I continued to love her. I prayed about our relationship and continued to try to get close to her, but her heart had hardened. Although I yearned for her attention, affection and love, we became like strangers. This experience started a new chapter in my young life and, at the age of 18, I left home, feeling unloved and empty. Not having my mother's love and affection caused an ache in my heart that would not heal; so I sought love elsewhere, settling for unhealthy relationships.

At this present moment, I'm thinking back to the times in my life when I dated and looked for love from a man that I really didn't know, but so desired to meet. At the time, my daydreams and night dreams, along with my misplaced emotions, often left me hoping to find true love. I wanted a man to fall madly in love with me, to respect me and marry me. We'd move into a white house with a white picket fence, have a couple of kids, go to church on Sundays, enjoy each other's family and friends, and, during the holiday season, invite them over for dinner and fun. As I remember them now, many of my dreams were just lies that I desperately tried to make come true.

Whether or not I was dating, I continued to dream about having a healthy, loving relationship. I still missed my mother's love so much! This kind of thinking caused me to ignore the signs of unhealthy relationships. I just hoped that, in time, things would get better. I began settling for what I didn't want—looking for love in all the wrong *faces*. In those relationships, when I was sexually involved, God would convict me and tell me that I shouldn't be having sex without being married. I was tormented by guilt and began praying for God to heal my heart that was broken because of what my mother's boyfriend had done. I prayed that He would help me stop looking for this love that I thought I would never find.

Eventually, the real truth broke my dreams into pieces; reality captured me and began to dictate to my heart and mind what was really happening. One day, during a time that I was dating someone, I suddenly heard a voice speaking to me: "Your desire isn't the man that you chose. Even though you know each other's names, addresses, phone numbers and friends; and even though you have sex as often as you can, he doesn't see you as a woman that prays and goes to church, and wants to settle down and get married. He sees and treats you like you let him treat you. He sees you and treats you as a nice sex partner, nothing more and nothing less." Realizing that obvious truth made me pause for a moment, then cry for a while. Finally, I exhaled and accepted it. I knew immediately that I had to pray for God to change my ways and give me strength to not just talk the talk, but live holy and wait for Him to send my husband to me.

Before this reality was made plain to me, I thought like so many other women think today—that by pleasing a man, and acting and performing the duties of a wife, including sex, you were showing that man how much you cared, and this kind of behavior would eventually cause him to want marriage. But I learned very quickly that having sex with the man I was dating—who would often way he "loved" me, "needed" me, "wanted" me, "missed" me, had to "have" me—wasn't any reason to think that he loved me to the point of wanting to be married to me. What he was saying beneath all those sweet-sounding words was simply, "I want to have sex with you." Of course, when he would say those sweet things, I would daydream about them and let my imagination run away. I would hear what he said but never intended—and I would see only the dream that I hoped would come true. But my dream was lying to me…again…as in so many other times. "Temporary feelings" and "temporary love" faded to the point that I literally felt unloved, misplaced, and empty inside…again.

Yet, the more I began to pray, the closer to God I grew. I had a strong desire to be holy and please Him. My mind began to change and I decided that I would no longer "settle." I wanted something better than what I had been accepting. I wanted God to send me a saved, God-fearing man—one who loved me unconditionally—one who wanted me to be his wife.

When I realized what I truly wanted, I made a major decision. I prayed that, until I was married, God would take away my desire for sex. With God's strength, I was delivered from this temptation and remained celibate for over five years. I also prayed to God about the situation with my mother. He helped me and I was able to forgive her. I simply assumed that she didn't know how to deal with my childhood horror and was hurting as well. In my late 20s, God had revealed to me that my mother had loved me in the best way she knew. Forgiving my mother and her ex-boyfriend was the beginning of my own healing from the pain they caused.

I began trusting that God would send me the husband I prayed for—but this was not as easy as I thought. The devil kept trying to tempt me and destroy me. For example—he once had someone I really cared about call me. This was a man I had dated for two years. Over the phone, his conversation sounded so good that I felt like I would melt. But God…! The enemy kept telling me that I could date an unsaved man and, if I spent time with him, he would eventually change. Well…the devil is a liar! Demons continually tried to make me miss what God had in store—by trying to tempt me, distract me, and take me out of God's will. But whenever this happened, I went directly into prayer—and God always kept me strong and safe.

So…Did I ever finally meet the husband I prayed for? Well, one day while I was washing dishes, I heard the Lord's voice tell me to "pray for a companion." His voice was so loud and clear that it surprised me and I began to question Him. He repeated: "Go and pray for a companion." I immediately went and prayed from my heart about what kind of husband I wanted God to send. Four months later, on Good Friday in 1999, at a bank during my lunch hour, I met him. We were married three-and-a-half months later and are *still* happily married! Both of us are pastors and love serving the Lord. Waiting on God to send the man that He wanted me to marry was so worth it!
I learned that, no matter what happens or what I have to go through, nobody can love me or heal me like the Lord. There is no love like His love!

Don't ever let a lack of love, or any harmful experience, cause you to become someone you aren't supposed to be. Don't settle for less. You're special to God and He always wants the best for you. Trust in Him! Wait on the Lord!

A DIAGNOSIS, NOT A DEATH SENTENCE

Caroline D. Parker

On a beautiful, hot day in June 2010, which, ironically, would have been my late parents' sixty-first wedding anniversary, I received one of the most difficult diagnoses a person could ever receive. Sitting in the doctor's office at the Hematology/Oncology Department of Allegiance Hospital in Jackson, Michigan, I truly had no clue as to what awaited me.

I felt like I had already been through an emotional war zone in the years since 1995, when my beloved Mama passed away. Her death had caused my world to implode and it would be years before I felt like the person I had been when she was alive. I had great difficulty adjusting to the new "normal" in my life. Mama was my touchstone and my other half; and for years after she died I felt crippled, lost, and useless. To compound the devastation, my siblings and I were left with caring for our father. Daddy and I had a very difficult relationship and had never connected in the way Mama and I did. Looking back now, I can see that I wasn't able to transcend my grief enough to care for my dad, and he eventually moved from the apartment we had shared with Mama to an assisted living facility. My sister took on most of the responsibility of caring for Daddy, but his health declined to the point where he went to a nursing home—a place he never wanted to be. Barely four years after Mama passed, Daddy died there; and for years, I felt yoked to a burden of guilt that I wasn't a better daughter to him.

So that day, June 18, 2010, as I sat alone in the examining room, I felt the full weight of the loss of my parents. The doctor came in, sat down, and informed me that he suspected the ailment which had sapped my strength so badly was cancer. I was more shocked than scared. In fact, when the doctor left briefly to schedule an immediate bone marrow biopsy of my breastplate, my shock erupted into righteous anger. Instead of being angry with God, I literally spoke to the devil as if he were there in person—as if I had him by the throat. I unleashed my anger on him without limit and without boundaries. I told him he would not take me out like this, and I would not die because of his attack. In retrospect, those few minutes alone were the best thing that came out of that day, because all the faith I had rose up inside me as I told the devil "no!"

The doctor returned and told me that my disease was such that my kidneys would "likely fail," and that my bones "likely had lesions on them." I would have to begin an immediate course of strong chemotherapy. As he spoke, I prayed in the Spirit under my breath and kept Satan's fiery darts at bay. When I questioned the doctor, he became irritated and told me he knew what was best for me because he had over 30 years of experience dealing with cancer. I felt I had no medical ally in this fight, and that was more discouraging than the diagnosis.

The office biopsy was "inconclusive" and I was scheduled for a round of tests—a skeletal x-ray survey, a "welcome to your cancer" therapy session, and the first of my twice-weekly chemo sessions. When I finally returned to my car,

I sat for a minute, called my closest cousin and told her we needed to pray.
As is her custom, she prayed immediately and encouraged me to have faith in God. Then, I had a conference call with my brother and sister to tell them the news and that I would keep them informed as I received information.

I have now completed my full round of treatment and the cancer is in full remission—against all odds. I totally believe—and I know—that it's because I have faith, and I used that faith to quench the fiery darts of Satan's wicked attack against me. Though I still have residual physical symptoms due to the intensity of the chemo, I am working hard to get my strength back and my life is wonderful.

During this tough journey, I learned three major things that transformed my life and strengthened my faith even more.

Let's begin with Number Three – Do Not Fear Death:
Months of twice-weekly chemotherapy wreaked havoc on my body. Often, I was so debilitated that I would weep in pain as I showered and got ready to go to the session—being sure that this time would be the one I couldn't endure. But God was with me, and I never missed one full-on session due to illness. During the first several weeks of chemo, my sleep pattern was not balanced and I would lie awake many nights feeling lonely, discouraged and sick. But in the midst of those dark times, the Holy Spirit sheltered me as I cried and suffered through the side effects. It was during those dark times that I truly faced the issue of my mortality. Though God promised me through a spiritual prophecy that I would live, sometimes I felt so sick and emotionally debilitated that I was ready to die. But as the chemo sessions progressed, I became less afraid of dying—and I learned this: Once we face death and accept

that we'll all leave this earth, either through death or the rapture, we destroy a weapon in Satan's arsenal against us. This is incredibly freeing in every other area of our lives; because under this realization, we can live unfettered by the primary fear we all have. I even lost my intense fear of flying, because what I faced in the dark helped me face daily life.

Number Two – God Has Our Back:
For the first 40+ years of my life, I had serious trust issues concerning God. I always believed He existed, but I grew up in a culture of religion that believed God punished you if you stepped out of line. I saw Him as unyielding and unmerciful; and at times I hated God, because I was blinded to who He really is. But God showed his love to me anyway and over time, I began to trust God and His Word more than my feelings. A major turning point in my life came two years after Daddy died. I was lying in bed—crying and miserable—and I asked God why my life was so difficult and unfulfilling. Immediately, a picture came into my mind—a large concrete field studded with pointed shards of colored glass. The Holy Spirit impressed upon me: "You have so much difficulty because your basic emotional foundation is littered with the fear that was set in your childhood." I was stunned at the truth of God's wisdom. He further said to me: "I will help you dig up your foundation. It will be painful, but if you trust Me, I will plant a new garden of faith within you."

Nine years later—though I still had inner work that needed to be done—God had reworked my "spiritual garden" to the point where I was able to stand strong in the face of that cancer diagnosis.

The Number One thing I had to do is: I had to forgive. Mama's death not only caused my emotional world to crash and burn, it wreaked havoc on my physical world as well. Though I had a good job and made good money, Daddy's death in 1999 put me in a financial bind. I owed over $16,000 in taxes as the beneficiary of his insurance, and even though I received the money, it was to be shared with my siblings. I alone had the burden of paying the taxes.

After this time, my life began to unravel and I felt I would never again have a stable life. When Daddy had moved and I couldn't afford the rent on our place, it had set in motion a fifteen-year cycle of being an itinerant.

The breaking point came at the last place I stayed when I discovered that some of my relatives were bad-mouthing me to other family and friends. A cousin, who was like a sister to me, stopped speaking to me and I was told I had to leave the place I was staying. I had nowhere to go at that point. But looking back, I see that God was pulling up the last of my "fear-filled" garden and re-seeding it with new fruit, though at that moment, I simply felt alone and unwanted. The only place I had left to go was a homeless shelter. I told the Lord I would go as long as He would quickly teach me whatever lessons I needed to learn. My, how we arrogantly barter with God when we have nothing to offer!

Even though I was scared and embarrassed, I settled in my heart that I would find a shelter and learn what God had for me. When my mind was set on doing so, I felt a calming peace come over me. Within days, I found that God had already worked out a living situation for me. At that moment, I knew how Abraham felt when the ram appeared to him.

Through a series of miraculous, amazing behind-the-scenes maneuvers—orchestrated by God, of course, I moved, rent free, into a rental home that my closest cousin had in Jackson, Michigan. She asked only that I pay the utilities. To this day, since I had no income or job, I do not know where the money came from; but I never missed one monthly payment. The faith seeds that God had planted in my garden were beginning to bloom; and I believe that God, knowing I'd face a cancer diagnosis, put me in Jackson to be cared for by the wonderful staff at Allegiance Hospital's Hematology/Oncology Department.

After my discouraging initial session with the first doctor, I found the other medical professionals to be caring and supportive. They inspired my faith walk, encouraging my belief in God's healing even as they administered my chemo. To this day, I am grateful to them for their care, kindness, and support.

But the most important "medicine" in my healing process was learning to forgive and let go of the hurts I experienced in my last living situation. When I first moved to Jackson, I had been so angry and hurt by what had happened that I let resentment bubble up in me. Three months after I moved, my health and emotions were still broken; but again, I now realize that these situations were part of God reworking my spiritual garden. The strain so impacted me that I developed shingles, which can be caused by high-stress situations.

As the shingles healed, and in the months before that fateful diagnosis, I had time to evaluate my feelings over my relatives' hurtful gossip. I purposed in my heart to forgive them—not with an "I'll forgive you but I won't forget" mentality, but with true forgiveness. When I talked to my sister, who is a minister, about how to truly forgive people, she said something that really helped me. She said: "You won't always get closure in every situation and some things you won't understand on this side. So, what do you really want: forgiveness…justice…retribution…what?" That opened up to me my true feelings about the situation. I realized that what I had wanted most was justice, and to ask them why they never spoke directly with me instead of behind my back. Once I admitted my true feelings and took them to the Lord in honesty and truth, I felt the burden lift from me. I learned that true forgiveness begins with honesty about what we feel, no matter how bad and/or ugly it may seem to us.

As I write this, my life is great. I still have some health challenges, but overall, I am at peace and loving life. I thank God for the journey so far, and I can't wait to see what's ahead!

THIS IS YOUR LIFE.
DO WHAT YOU LOVE,
AND DO IT OFTEN.
IF YOU DON'T LIKE SOMETHING, CHANGE IT.
IF YOU DON'T LIKE YOUR JOB, QUIT.
IF YOU DON'T HAVE ENOUGH TIME, STOP WATCHING TV.
IF YOU ARE LOOKING FOR THE LOVE OF YOUR LIFE, STOP;
THEY WILL BE WAITING FOR YOU WHEN YOU
START DOING THINGS YOU LOVE.
STOP OVER ANALYZING,
LIFE IS SIMPLE.
ALL EMOTIONS ARE BEAUTIFUL.
WHEN YOU EAT, APPRECIATE
EVERY LAST BITE.
OPEN YOUR MIND, ARMS, AND HEART TO NEW THINGS
AND PEOPLE, WE ARE UNITED IN OUR DIFFERENCES.
ASK THE NEXT PERSON YOU SEE WHAT THEIR PASSION IS,
AND SHARE YOUR INSPIRING DREAM WITH THEM.
TRAVEL OFTEN; GETTING LOST WILL
HELP YOU FIND YOURSELF.
SOME OPPORTUNITIES ONLY COME ONCE, SEIZE THEM.
LIFE IS ABOUT THE PEOPLE YOU MEET, AND
THE THINGS YOU CREATE WITH THEM
SO GO OUT AND START CREATING.
LIFE IS SHORT.
LIVE YOUR DREAM,
AND WEAR
YOUR PASSION.

CANCER IS NOT A DEATH SENTENCE: A Sister's Perspective

Evangelist Valerie M. Robinson

Cancer…the very word evokes a myriad of emotions. Cancer strikes fear in the core of the most ardent and invincible heart. Cancer…at the mention of the word, one feels an assault to the senses. Cancer…it means "a fight to the finish."

Fear, dread, doubt, unbelief, a sense of loss, uncertainty, helplessness, hopelessness and anger are the tentacles of emotions attached to the word "cancer"—even for those who are bystanders, pondering its implications. I've never been diagnosed with cancer, but my walk through the challenge with my sister Caroline, as she made her journey from diagnosis to deliverance, has given me a unique perspective on the lives of those who face this same malady. I've come to realize that a cancer diagnosis affects both the patient and the patient's loved one; and it is my prayer, as you read this story, that you will know God loves you…He is rooting for you…He's making intercession for you as you go through your storm. He wants you to know "this too shall pass."

God teaches lessons to both the patient and their loved one who must walk this road. I know, beyond the shadow of a doubt, that God loves us and wants the best for His children. Through this process of support, I learned that He wants his children healed, set free and delivered just as much, if not more, than His children want it for themselves—so much so that He staked His very life on it.

My story is for those who have to walk through the valley of the shadow of cancer with a loved one. It isn't a walk I would have chosen for my sister or our family, but in hindsight, the path was one that GOD used to show us His awesome healing power. As an ordained minister, this journey showed me that faith to be healed isn't just for those who are on the preaching platforms of the world, but it's for every believer who loves God and trusts Him unconditionally.

My siblings and I made a pact that we would keep each other abreast of major happenings in our lives. As adults, we have come to cherish each other and I can't imagine life without my sister and brother. The love I have for my siblings and their children can never be put into words. My love for God, my husband Melvin, my daughter Chelsea and the family I grew up with at 4157 Moore Street, encompasses everything about me; and I am forever grateful to God to have all of them in my life.

My sister had not been well for over a year, but in spite of her physical challenges, she had maintained a sustaining faith during a very critical period in her life. I know she had dark days and periods of suffering in silence…days when she thought it would be better to "go home and be with Jesus"…and other days where she wondered, "Why?" There were days when she was strong, could pray Heaven down and rebuke the devil; and then there were days when she would just let me pray, then softly say "Amen" at the end of the prayer. But it wasn't until I received a call at work that I realized this was not going to be "business as usual."

It was mid-afternoon on June 18, 2010, when Caroline called me at work and she asked if I could do a three-way call with our brother Daniel who lived out of state. She wanted us both to hear what the doctor told her. After the usual greetings, Caroline began to speak to us: "Well, I've just come back from my doctor's appointment and he told me I have multiple myeloma, which is a cancer of the bloodstream." I remember saying, "The devil is a liar; the blood of Jesus supersedes that!"—and my brother softly agreeing—and Caroline saying, " I know that's right!" But what struck me most—and what would be Caroline's mantra throughout the entire journey of deliverance—was what she said then: "This is the doctor's diagnosis, not mine!" I would come to believe that these words she uttered weren't said just to make her appear to be a super-saint, but they would be the talk-path of the Holy Spirit as He led her and our family during this journey of faith. "Lord, I believe. Help thou my unbelief."

After telling us the "doctor's diagnosis," Caroline informed us of what appointments she would have in determining her best course of action for treatment. After we ended the call, I remember feeling a split between my soul (my emotions) and my spirit. I became increasingly aware that I am a three-part being: spirit, soul and body, and that my body simply reacted to what was taking place in the realm of my spirit and my soul. I recall telling the Lord that I knew He is the Healer, and that He had already delivered Caroline, but I needed to have His promise fixed within my heart and mind…for His work was already done.

On the Sunday following Caroline's news, I was scheduled to attend a "family and friends" service; and even though I was still wrestling with her diagnosis, I knew I had to be at church. Whenever I felt weak, I had been telling the Lord that I needed help with my flesh. In my spirit-man, I knew that God is able to heal; but in my flesh, I was afraid and needed to gain more control.

I went to service that Sunday with an inward struggle. But I knew that, as a worshipper, my worship doesn't stop because things in my life aren't conducive to praise. I have learned to bless the Lord at all times, even during the not-so-good times that He allows in my life. Actually, our worship has to become even more intense during the times we are in battle. And that day, even though Satan's attacks against my mind were like rounds from an AK-47 assault rifle, I continued to worship and praise God. I had to rebuke and cast down the ungodly imaginations and thoughts that were being thrown my way.

I heard an awesome, anointed word through the ministry of Bishop Tudor Bismark—and I had a wonderful time in the Lord's presence—but still my heart was heavy. If I was going to be a support to my sister, I had to get my own mind and heart in the right state…and I knew I needed help with that.

I thank God for the wonderful men and women He has put in my life. I have been blessed to meet and develop covenant relationships with some very powerful, Spirit-filled people of God. I am forever grateful to Pastors Joe and Velma Biggers, Pastor Cheryl Swanigan and Pastor Angela Prado of Embassy Covenant Church. God used them to help usher me into a realm of faith where the flesh had to die and be subject to God's power.

After the service, I went to greet these wonderful friends, but as I walked towards them, I began to break down inside. Pastor Joe Biggers, whom I call my "Big Brother," gave me a bear hug as he asked, "What is wrong with you?" Crying uncontrollably, I was soon surrounded by men and women of God, and I poured out the dreaded news about Caroline. Immediately, they began to pray and intercede together; and as they prayed, I felt the Lord's presence over me. I went down on my face…on the floor…still sobbing uncontrollably.

But it was there…on the floor…that the most amazing thing happened. I no longer heard the praying around me, but I began to hear God's voice—clear and strong in my spirit. God told me, "Get all of your crying out while you are on this floor, because when you get up there will be no more tears. You have to be ready to war." I really can't tell you how long I cried on the floor; but I can tell you that when I was able to move and get up, it was as if I had sprouted two large angel wings in my back. I came up off the floor with a power I had never before felt. I was a totally different person! I stood up and said, "I am ready!" Pastor Cheryl began to give me advice and strategies about what to look for during the healing process. I shook my head affirmatively as she spoke, but I was concentrating more on the work the Lord had done in me. I remember telling her, "I'm good! I just needed to get the flesh off of me and out of my way!"

My sister's chemo treatment became a means through which God revealed His character, His humor and His attention…in even the tiniest of details. For instance, Caroline's hair never fell out as is typical with cancer patients. Instead, her hair grew longer—below her shoulders. There were days when Caroline called me as she went through the treatments—and she would be witnessing to those receiving treatments around her. She would say, "I want to go through all of the experiences I need to go through so I will be able to say that God brought me through each stage of the healing process."

A bone marrow transplant was prescribed by her doctors. She would endure this process at the Karmanos Cancer Center in Detroit, Michigan. As her sister, I never wanted Caroline to go through the transplant. However, I'd always told her that I would honor her health decisions; so in support, I agreed to accompany her to the Cancer Center for her consultation appointment. The pivotal moment…the memorable moment…the defining moment of God's grace and mercy…was when the doctor announced to us that no bone marrow treatment would be needed. In fact, there was no sign that cancer was present in her body! She was free to go! She was…cancer-free!!

You'll be happy to know that we kept a modicum of decorum as we had a "Hallelujah!" PRAISE BREAK in that examination room. We praised God…thanking Him and dancing before Him that He brought us all through that emotional, mental, spiritual and physical journey of healing.

Beloved, God is able to give you peace. He is able to give you a praise and supernatural staying power to get you to an expected end. I can't tell you the entire story on these few pages, but this one thing I've learned: When God does something wonderful for you, don't WITHHOLD your praise! Where he SHOWS UP, you SHOW OUT in your praise, for He is truly an incredible God.

Dear Reader, I will end this story with a question. When words of death, disease or defeat are given, will you choose to believe and give life to the words of a negative report, or will you choose to believe the Word and report of the Lord? Which words will leap from the page and become your reality? God is asking, "Whom shall believe our report and to whom has the arm of the Lord been revealed?" Isaiah 53:1. Let's choose to believe the report of the Lord, for He is faithful!

BREAK THROUGH THE WALLS OF THIS WORLD

Pastor O. Agnes Kgasoe

You may be experiencing some difficult challenges in your life. Maybe you are presently going through some discouraging times. Unhealthy family background, unstable conditions in life and many different situations and economic instabilities have certainly affected people of all ages. Many have lost hope. They have lost their hard-earned properties and homes. Relationships have been strained. We have all been tested.

But in the midst of these difficult times, know that God's plan is presently at work in your life. In Jeremiah 29:11 (NIV), God says, "For I know the plans I have for you, plans to prosper you and not to harm you, plans to give you hope and future." At times, through our weaknesses and unbelief, we give up so easily...before we discover God's plan for our lives.

My heart's desire through sharing my life's testimony is to encourage you to stand up against all odds. You have the seeds of greatness planted within you by the hand of God. Your best days are still ahead. My prayer is one of encouragement—to enlarge your vision so you might find the courage to overcome any hindrance in your life and accomplish your God-given dreams and purpose.

I am the first-born child in a family of seven. We were raised by my grandmother, as my mother was a domestic worker and stayed in Johannesburg most of the time. We rarely spent time together with her as a family—only at times during school holidays. We were so accustomed to being with my grandmother that she truly grew to be an "adopted mother" to us. And so, it became natural for us to refer to her as our real "mother."

Due to tradition in the olden days, it was acceptable for parents to arrange traditional marriages for their children without their children's consent. My mother, at a very early age, experienced just that. Her parents forced her into a traditional marriage to a man she never loved. Five children were born from this abusive relationship. I was the first-born and four siblings followed. As my mother grew older and gained self-confidence, she became aware of the unfairness and abuse she was subjected to. On her own, she left this man and took us to my grandmother's home to live. She left for Johannesburg to look for work and we stayed with my grandmother until she died in 1976. We then began living with my aunt.

As these unhealthy situations were happening, the victims who suffered the most severe negative repercussions were me and my siblings. We were never well cared for and the environment in which we grew was not good. Our confidence in living life and fulfilling our aspirations for the future was severely handicapped. We simply lived each day as it came...merely surviving...going forward to the next day. But I know that if God has a purpose for your life, no one can stop it. Though we were ignorant of God s involvement in our lives, He never left us alone. His protection was always with us.

By age sixteen, another negative incident occurred in my life. The same fate that my mother experienced nearly happened to me. A man far older than me attempted to convince my family that he should marry me—in the traditionally "arranged" fashion. His family, through his mother, approached my aunt about her son's intentions to marry me. Because my mother was in Johannesburg and unable to give her consent, my aunt could not make a decision. She wrote my mother a letter about the matter, but as all this commotion was happening, I was suspicious of the situation. I could see and feel the secrecy associated with this woman's visits at home. I approached my aunt, and when I inquired as to what was going on, she was open with me and let me know about this man's intentions to marry me. She also made it clear to me that the matter had nothing to do with me. It was a matter for the elders to decide. I was frustrated...fearful...my heart full of hopelessness. I silently decided that if this became acceptable to my mother, I would commit suicide.

Because God intervened on my behalf, my mother's reply came as clear and decisive to my aunt. "Tell that family, to back off from my daughter. I know what I went through. My daughter is still in school, and when the right time comes for her marriage, she'll decide for herself about the matter." This answer came as a blow to many family members. I discovered that many of them were aware of this situation. Bad things were said and bad wishes were thrown at us, because refusing a marriage proposal was "taboo" in the area.

Later in life, we moved to a small house in another nearby village. My mother, now legally married to someone she loved, was still living in Johannesburg with our step-father. My siblings and I were living on our own. I was both "big sister" and "parent." Life was really tough, and literally everything was scarce. Money was limited...food was limited...but we had to survive. During this time, I was completing my Junior Certificate Class. After completing my courses at the end of the year, I had to proceed to another school for further studies. Unfortunately, my parents were not aware of any of this. I had to fend for myself in terms of being admitted to school, buying books, and getting money for registration and travel. By God's grace, I was admitted at a commercial high school in Rustenburg. A family friend provided money for my registration, and later, my parents became involved.

The path of studies I took at the school was regarded as the lowest. Fellow students would tease us that we were being trained for the lowest career in the workforce. But I succeeded in my studies, and a few months after I went back home, I was hired as a private teacher at a middle school. During this time, I registered for a one-year "Teacher's Training" course, which I completed in 1988.

I later married my wonderful husband, who encouraged me to continue my studies. So, in 1994, I took a "study leave" for four years and studied for a Bachelor of Arts degree with Vista University in Pretoria. After obtaining it within three years, I studied further for a Bachelor of Arts (Honors Degree) with the University of Pretoria, and completed it in 1997.

Throughout my life, God has always been in control—directing my steps. During my formative years, with all the challenges facing me, no one could imagine these great achievements being associated with my life! I was the best student at the university. In fact, I was an assistant lecturer for some years at Vista University, and I am now the Associate Pastor of a great flourishing church. I am a business woman in charge of two fast-growing entities. I am a loyal wife to a loving, supportive husband. I am a mother raising two lovely daughters. In the church, God has given us many spiritual sons and daughters, and we strive to be their living role models.

God is, indeed, good all the time. I lack enough words to encourage you to truly trust in Him. I know that God will never disappoint you. I believe every life has no limits. Regardless of the challenges you meet, through God you can make it. In all the odds I faced, I never gave up. Low self-esteem, lack of proper parental care, poverty at home, and abusive traditional practices—they never deprived me. God helped me throughout. Even though my mother's salary was small when she began working, today, thanks to God, all her children are graduates and are successful. They have their own families and are impacting the lives of many people. So, get out of the box! Refuse to go down and be counted! You are born with a gift, and the tools are in your hand! You came to this world holding something special, so release it and allow God to unfold it.

"And he said unto me, 'My grace is sufficient for thee: for my strength is made perfect in weakness.' Most gladly therefore will I rather glory in my infirmities, that the power of Christ may rest upon me." 2 Corinthians 12: 9 (KJV). His power can manifest best in those who are weakest. Your power is mightily great because you are mightily weak. God loves weak people, so do not deny your weaknesses. Just allow God to use them to reveal His strength through you. Gideon's weakness was self-esteem and deep insecurities, but God transformed him into a mighty man of valor (Judges 6:12). The chosen heroes of this earth have been in the minority. God specializes in using the faithfulness of people with no special talents or gifts to turn the world upside down. Be encouraged!

LOVING YOU IS WRONG! I'VE GOT TO GET IT RIGHT!

Pastor Kimberly Brown

Marrying the "wrong" person whom you feel is the "right" person can be a very complicated situation, especially when it comes to dealing with it in the "church." It can be very confusing to receive clarity and direction on what to do in a marriage that isn't working…a marriage that is far from the biblical definition of what a Godly marriage should be. No one wants "divorce" to be a part of their story. It is my prayer that through my journey, God will help heal your pain and give you the courage needed—not to do the right thing because you think it's the right thing to do, but rather to recognize when God is bringing deliverance in your life from toxic and un-biblical strongholds. So, please understand that this message is not from an unforgiving heart, but rather from one that is whole. I wish no ill to anyone, nor do I want to add to the deplorable divorce rate in our world. I only want to echo that what God wants for you is good, and that with God's grace, rightly dividing His Word, and proper spiritual counsel, you too can go free!

The Journey

In the winter of 1960, at the turn of the decade, I was born to wonderful parents, whom I later learned to truly love and appreciate. My mother was educated—a God-fearing, gentle but strong woman; and my father was a Veteran of World War II and The Korean War. He was self-educated, because life demanded that he get out and work. Because of his own desire to have pursued his education beyond the 8th

grade, he always instilled in me the value of education. My father was a self-taught reader and writer, and he loved numbers with a passion. I would often watch him sit in his favorite chair, in the kitchen nook, and budget out his bills that lay on the table. This is where my mom made sure we'd have a sit-down meal every weekday and on Sundays. On the table were his calculator, his glasses (that he and mom shared), and his notebook filled with numbers. He had many sayings, and one of them came from the value he placed on education. He'd say, "Get your education so you can make sure you always have something to fall back on. Love a man, but never become so dependent that you can't take care of yourself if something doesn't work out." He must have been a prophet before his time and I, of course, didn't realize it. But out of the many things I didn't glean, because of my own anger and rebellion, I somehow managed to get that nugget.

My father was born in Little Rock, Arkansas, the son of a preacher. He took a turn away from his upbringing and sank into a life of alcoholism. He and my mom were married almost 60 years. My eldest brother, whom I loved, unfortunately became a victim of the cycle of addiction within my family and died at the age of forty. Then there I was—intelligent and spirited, but challenged. I too was drawn into the spiral of rebellion and addiction. My disdain for my father, being there but not being there, due to his addiction, turned to internal turmoil. I promised myself that when I married, I'd never marry anyone like him. I missed his goodness, which seemed shadowed by the dark cover of alcohol. It would be later, and through the eyes of Christ, that I could clearly see and cherish the gift he was to me.

As I stated, my mother was the "glue" in our family. She was a strong silent force that, with such grace, held it together. She worked and buffered her family from the ills of addiction. How did she do it? I later came to know that it was because of God...only God. You see, she took me to the "formal church," and made certain that I learned there was a power greater than I. Unlike some modern-day mothers, she would say, "If you don't go to church, you're not going anywhere." So I went, and God made an impact on my young heart there, up until the age of twelve. I would even say that God was my best friend. I was eight years younger than my brother and a year and a half ahead in school, so it was like being the only child. I remember even having an angelic visitation at age 8, but because I was propelled early into a life of perplexity and doubt, I turned away from my best friend, and delved into a life of dismay.

But God! At age fifteen, I had a profound encounter with Jesus Christ and began to live a transformed life. He gave me a passion for Him and his work, and through his Word, this rebellious girl became an obedient daughter. Through His love, generational cycles of addiction and confusion begin to break off from my life...or so it seemed. Naturally, seeking to honor Him was an interest in my life. I began to value my parents and their struggles in a different way, and I knew that one day, I too would be married for a life time it seemed.

In February 1982, my life would take on a new dynamic...marriage. I met and fell in love with who I thought was the "right man." I later came to understand that he never really loved me. As a woman—and a preacher at that—I wanted so desperately for my marriage and family to emulate that of "Ephesians 5:21" and "I Corinthians 13." Surely this was God's plan for my marriage and was the "right thing." What I didn't understand was that this image couldn't be mine alone; it must be my husband's as well. And so the journey began. Three blessed and highly gifted children were born to our union, the latter being over a decade apart from the first two.

As time would lay out the tale of lovelessness, no amount of prayers seemed to fix the disdain, or heal the hurt of his childhood, or correct the fact that I was just "not her." So it began with verbal slanders, degrading tones and then a hit or two on the head—added along with the complexities of emotional triangles and detachment. I had a husband "on paper" and "by night," but I felt like a married wife without a husband…left uncovered…left alone at the plays, at the parent conferences, at the graduations…alone in life, or so it felt. But I stayed with him...after all, it was the right thing to do; and after almost 60 years, that's what my mother had done…and her mother before her…and her mother before her…

In spite of my struggle between love and wanting to please God and worrying about what others thought, the cycle of abuse continued. I was an educated, God-fearing woman—a preacher! This could not be my story! Didn't I realize the situation? Weren't there enough signs or information? But I could only see my babies…my man…that I wanted love for a lifetime…that this was the right thing to do. I even got away for over a year, went to school and obtained my master's degree. I still desperately wanted to have my marriage be what I felt God wanted it to be—"till death us do part." I returned home. We had our third child and, for a moment, it was the best time; but the dream turned into a nightmare, only becoming worse. Could a person hate what they said they loved so much? It was a tangled web of women, words, blows, walking on eggshells, the threat of the shotgun, until…

One day, in the spring of 1998, the grace of God kicked in. Through appropriate counsel, prayer and fasting, my thinking shifted and I realized that God was not calling me to death, but to life! I found the courage to overcome public opinion and the false beliefs that I carried. I found courage through my dad's words; and most of all I found courage through the Word and peace of God. I packed up my children and a few things, and with peace and assurance in my heart, I left. I was free! I finally came to understand that God was not punishing me or requiring me to continue living in an abusive marriage.

I embraced God's Word with passion and I knew that God's plans for me were good and that my future would be bright. No more chains binding me! He set me free!

THE BUCK STOPS HERE

Minister Mary Edwards

CANCER! First my mother…then my brother…followed by my sister…all in 18 months. Whew! Finally…I had a breather…but only for two years before my beloved husband was stricken.

Prior to my late husband's departure, we had been community activists in Detroit for over 30 years. He loved Detroit and everyone knew it. So often we heard him say, "I was born here, raised here, and I will die here."

Strangely enough, following his retirement in 2002, he said, "I believe I can leave Detroit now." We were all amazed. Rev. Eddie K. Edwards had been a Michiganian of the Year, received a Presidential Award for his community service work, and was highly regarded by the city, county, and state governments for his commitment to Michigan. Most of our family also lives here, and this sudden change of heart was hard for us to understand. Nevertheless, in December 2003, we began to make plans to relocate to Texas. I could never understand why we were moving to Texas, except that Eddie loved horses, western apparel and western hats. That didn't seem like a good enough reason, but I would have gone to the ends of the earth with him. At that point, we had been married for 21 years…and I was accustomed to him making good decisions. He was just that kind of guy.

During that Christmas season, we looked for a home in Texas. It didn't take long for us to find a lovely one, and negotiations on the purchase began, pending the sale of our Detroit home. We rushed back and put our home on the market. The real estate agent we worked with felt sure our home would sell quickly. She would smile from ear to ear as she watched the pleasure on faces of the house hunters and listened to their remarks. We were all surprised after 30 people looked at the home and, even though many expressed their love for it, not one of them put a bid on it. Thank God they didn't.

In March 2004, Eddie began to complain about having a pain in his side. At first, the doctor diagnosed it as an infection and gave him a prescription for antibiotics, which he took for about a month. When his condition didn't improve, he had a biopsy. That's when we discovered that he was in stage four of cancer and had only four to six months of life remaining! He was a health-conscious person and it was difficult for us to understand how his condition could develop to stage four with us not realizing that was terribly wrong. In July 2004, Eddie left this life, just five months after his diagnosis.

My husband's passing left me in a state of utter shock, making the important decisions alone. But the transition from wife to widow wasn't the only major crisis I had to deal with. Barely before I could catch my breath, I WAS DIAGNOSED WITH CANCER. I had always been faithful to have mammograms on a consistent basis, but when I had my annual mammogram this time, the test showed "something abnormal" on the film. I needed to have a biopsy, which I did. The biopsy results told me that I had stage one of breast cancer! Naturally, I was panic-stricken...and images of death began to dance in my head. I thought about my mother, my brother, my sister, and my husband—all dying from this awful disease.

I managed to rise above my initial fears, and began to prepare myself for battle. I had always been a fighter…and that's a good thing…because now, I was fighting for my OWN life and the lives of my grandchildren and great grandchildren. ENOUGH IS ENOUGH! I refused to sit by idly and watch this deadly disease take the lives of me and my offspring.

Being a writer with a very creative imagination, I immediately began to see myself healed—not dead. Instead of writing out my obituary, I wrote out my goals for the next five years. And I wrote my autobiography! I designed and posted signs all over my home for my eyes to see. One said: "THE BUCK STOPS HERE!" Here is another sign—an image that I've shared with others who are going through the challenges of cancer. I hope it will help someone else.

When it came time for my scheduled surgery, I can truthfully say that all fear was gone. Although I had to go back twice for the disease to be removed, (it was so small that it was hard to pinpoint), it was removed on an outpatient basis!

Looking back, I am not only grateful to God that my life was spared, but I learned a tremendous lesson from this defining moment in my life—the importance of praying the right prayer. Eddie and I never asked God's permission to leave Detroit. What we prayed was that God would bless us to sell our home and move to Texas. Now, it's clear to me how devastating it would have been had we left Detroit, leaving all our family and friends (especially our grandchildren). I would have been like a ship without a sail. Also disturbing is the thought that, had we moved, I would have never begun my widows' ministry here in Detroit, where I have had the opportunity to serve hundreds of widows.

Yes, it's true that I've lost my dear mother, ALL of my siblings, and my late husband to cancer. But today, I'm cancer-free and the buck stops here! I am the only member of my immediate family still living today after being stricken with this disease—and I plan to live a long time—and finish the story!

WHERE HE LOVES US

Rebecca S. Bailey

With the Roe v Wade anniversary energizing an anti-abortion initiative within our church, I found myself reflecting on my own "surprise" pregnancy years ago. As with any other happening in our lives, the sharpness of the pain had faded over the years. But though I elected to take a passive stance regarding abortion, the Lord shook those thoughts from my memory and caused me to recount, in graphic detail, the choice I had made.

The image in my memory I had set aside long ago—the telltale glow of a "blue plus" sign; but now those thoughts vividly came back to me. I was 20 years old and pregnant.

Holding the test stick, I sat for a few moments, feeling an overwhelming feeling of fear and dread. What would I do? What should I do? My parents would be furious—and my siblings would never understand. Most of my friends were churchgoers and I knew they would judge me either way. I was in trouble and I was desperate.

I pondered abortion. I was still very early in my pregnancy—probably about 4 weeks along. The idea of being pregnant was revolting and I immediately tried to picture an image of carrying a child to full-term, then surrendering through adoption. The stress and anxiety was unbearable. I wept as I told my boyfriend of the dilemma...hoping against hope that he would decide we should be married...longing for him to want a family with me. But his response was, "I'll pay for an abortion." I was devastated.

Ever a man pleaser, I made an appointment, hoping he would stop me. He said he simply did not want a child. He said we were too young. He would pay for the procedure and would drive me to the clinic. He would wait in the waiting room and drive me home afterwards. He loved me…so he said. But the thought burned in my mind: "How, if he loved me, could he ask me to betray everything I had believed in?" I tried to be brave. I tried to not let the flood of thoughts of rejection and abandonment overwhelm me.

In the clinic, I was handed a valium…as though a pill would help me escape my beliefs and think that what I was about to do was not wrong…was not heinous…was not sin. I sat in a hospital gown…in a chair…surrounded by 5 or 6 women "like me." We were all there for one reason. I studied each face and wondered about their apathy. I had not stopped tearing up since I arrived, but perhaps their valium was working, I thought.

As my name was called, I was led into an examining room. Lying back, feet in stirrups, I looked up at the ceiling as two attendants asked me if I was comfortable. Comfortable? Idiot women! They placed a sheet over my legs to afford me a sense of modesty. The doctor walked in…cool, distant, and almost rude. He reassured me this procedure was safe. The child, he said, was not a child…only a ball of flesh no bigger than my thumbnail…unremarkable, in fact. No heartbeat…no thoughts…no nerve endings. He used a speculum and opened my cervix. The whining noise of the vacuum started and I instinctively turned away from him and began to cry. He stopped for a moment and asked if I wanted to continue.

I had no choice, I thought. I was trapped, exposed, unloved, abandoned, and worthless. I nodded for him to just get it done. The attendant held my hand and tears rolled down my cheeks as I felt the tearing of flesh from flesh.

My baby was gone.

The doctor disentangled me from the equipment, removed his rubber gloves and walked out without the slightest regard for the incredible violation he had just performed...or maybe that is why he walked away so quickly.

I was allowed to rest for a few moments until the bleeding slowed, then moved into a recovery room where I sat in a reclining chair, bundled in a blanket. A large black woman sat next to me, and between us was a small service table that held a pitcher and some glasses.

Eyes blurry from tears, I stared at the floor and tried to grasp the ordeal I had gone through. I tried to comprehend what had just happened. I tried to shove my anger and sadness deep into the pit of my soul, never to be revisited.

"May I serve you some juice?" the woman asked softly. I glanced up into her brown eyes. They were kind, compassionate and understanding. I stared into those "soul windows" feeling a strange sense of comfort in such a stark and unloving place. After a moment, I nodded "yes" and thanked her. As she poured my glass and handed it to me, she looked at me again, studying the tears running down my cheeks, and asked gently, "Why did you do it?"

I struggled for an answer but none seemed adequate. None seemed valid. "Why" was the question I had been asking of myself…and I simply did not have an adequate answer. Because my boyfriend didn't want a child? Because I was too young? Because I had no money? Because I was unmarried? None of the answers could fully justify my decision. So I said nothing.

The woman waited a few moments and said, "My husband and me got 6 kids. We can't afford no more." She waited for my response but I just looked at her speechless. "Why did you?" she asked again.

"My boyfriend doesn't want a baby." My throat constricted and I struggled to maintain my composure, but my countenance crumpled and I began to sob.

Firmly, but again gently, she replied, "You shouldn't have done it for him." She was gentle and quiet. We sat together, though we did not speak again.

As I recalled this 20-year-old experience in such explicit detail, long-forgotten tears of grief came back to me. The sadness, hurt and anger bubbled to the surface, and for the first time since that terrible day, I wept for the child I would never know. I imagined a girl…her face like mine…blonde and blue-eyed…with my mother's smile. My baby girl would have been intelligent, fun loving and artistic, like so many in my family…maybe even athletic…or perhaps "bookish." I continued to sob…pouring out the years of pent up and long-suppressed grief. There was something more to the incident than I had realized before…

Though it was a terrible time of callous treatment when I was confused, scared, trapped and unloved, I can now look back at the scenario and see the gentle hand of Yahweh through a woman who offered me juice…who gently spoke to me…who was kind and compassionate in a moment when I was in great need.

Like so many others, I had wrestled with the question of whether a zygote is a life instead of wrestling with the root of the issue…a sinful nature that corrupts everything…even the womb. I had hidden behind legalism, semantics and justification…because the alternative is just too devastating. If I could only believe the zygote is not a real life, then I have killed no one. Now, though, I was being asked by Yahweh to choose a side in this argument…to review my history…to confess my sin. I needed to admit what I had done; and oh, how painful and frightening a guilty plea before our Righteous Judge can be!

But in the midst of this repentance, it occurred to me that Yahweh, with infinite mercy and kindness, had dealt with me even before I came to this moment. There had been no lecture to abstain. There was no argument over the right or wrong of the issue. There was only the kindness of a woman who suffered too. There was only the gentle voice of compassion that resonates in my heart even now. There was only the soft touch of a hand that held mine as we reclined in our chairs and sipped juice. I know that in that dark place of an abortion clinic, I had been accompanied by Yashua Ha Messiah, who, in a stark and barren recovery room, had loved me right there.
I can no longer remain passive in response to such love…His love.

DEAR...

Michele Sweeting-DeCaro

I married my husband, Lou, in June 2000. He was 43 and I was 35. As an "older" couple, we knew getting pregnant could be risky, so we didn't want to wait too long. When the first year passed with no baby, we became more vigorous in our attempts. But another year passed, and still—no baby. We sought medical attention, discovering that Lou's sperm had a low motility rate; and as a result, he received medication, followed by an outpatient procedure, in hopes of rectifying the problem. But three years passed, still—no baby. As people of faith and involved in church ministry, we prayed daily about being parents and believed God would make a way. Four years passed—no baby, and then five years passed—STILL—no baby. Even after Lou's procedure, we knew something was seriously wrong. But I managed to put on a "smiling" persona—even in the face of the countless comments from sincere family and friends: "When are you two going to have a baby?" I'd grin and respond, "We're enjoying our lives right now"—when, on the inside, I was drowning in a sea of sadness. I cried every night—asking God, "Why? Why me?" Lou continued to lovingly encourage me: "Don't worry," he would say; but as much as I wanted to trust his words, my worry took over.

Now let me explain here that "worry," for me, means writing. I love writing, particularly free writing...pouring my prayers, thoughts, questions, and frustrations out on paper. It's cathartic. I always keep a journal chronicling my experiences—sort of a "working memory," checking back every couple of months to look for progress. Studies show that translating an experience into language makes that experience lucid and transparent. In other words, you literally see your words and can experience healing. I needed healing and answers, so I wrote: "Dear _______: Why? What is going on? Why am I not able to have a child?"

I made an appointment to see a fertility specialist, not realizing how expensive and extensive the process was. The doctor felt sorry for us as she watched my eyes well up with tears, and the lump in my throat prevent me from speaking. She gave me a "courtesy check-up" and saw three fibroids the size of oranges pressed against my uterus. What! My doctor had said they were "pea-sized" and "caused no issues." She carefully moved the ugly "problem" and told us to try again. This was in March 2005.

A month later, early in the morning, Lou was in the bathroom when he felt a warm sensation, like a liquid drop, hit his back. It seemed strange to him, and he inspected the ceiling for a leak, but found nothing. Lou dismissed the experience and shortly forgot about it. But we are people of prayer, and in retrospect, while we have no proof, we do believe that something very spiritual happened there that morning.

It was May 2005 when I missed my period. I'd missed my period before, so I didn't get my hopes up. But I heard a whisper, as if someone stood behind me, saying, "Don't worry." I ignored it, but we decided to take the day off, go to the doctor, and take a pregnancy test. And just like that, after five long years, we discovered that we were pregnant! Everyone was elated, but no one more thrilled than me. God had answered my prayers; and, even though I was considered "older," I would have a beautiful, healthy baby—and I would no longer worry, but I would write: "Dear _______: Don't worry. I'm 39 and joyfully pregnant with disturbing fibroids. Help me not to fret."

Having fibroids made pregnancy extremely painful and made my tummy look bigger than usual as the three fibroids grew to the size of melons...ouch! Early on, I was told that I had a "high risk" pregnancy, so I stopped working, kept my feet up, and watched "baby" programs. I also enjoyed reading the biblical account of Sarah, who bore her son at 90 years old. "Dear _______: Don't worry. If Sarah can give birth at 90, I'm in good hands."

I was a month shy of 40 years old when Loumike (LM) was born in January 2006. He was the most beautiful child we'd ever seen. LM's smile and constant giggle were infectious in our home. At about six months old, his first word was "Dada." We were ecstatic. But as time went on, LM began missing major milestones in his development. At two years old, we called LM "the slider" because of the way he moved around on his butt instead of walking. "Dear _______: Don't worry. He just babbles and says 'Dada.' I'm scared."

On a sunny June afternoon in 2008, after LM spent almost an hour silently lining up his toy cars on the kitchen counter, he began opening and closing all the kitchen cabinet doors. I turned and spoke to Lou:
"He has Autism."
"What?"
"Autism."
"I don't think so. Let's hear what the doctor has to say."

LM's two-year check-up with his pediatrician had been scheduled for the next day, so it was the perfect time to address my concerns. "I wouldn't worry too much since boys have a tendency to start slower than girls in many areas of development," the doc said. I breathed a sigh of relief, but still had a battle within. I just felt in my spirit that something was "off" with my only child, for whom I had waited so long. Yet, still lingering in the depth of my soul was that voice, "Don't worry." Time to start writing again…

LM was finally walking at two and a half years when we enrolled him in the daycare center at our apartment complex. We hoped that, by being around other children, his language would emerge. For the first month, he cried every day, but the teacher insisted everything would be fine. By the second month, LM fit in—but still no talking. The teachers loved LM and encouraged him to play with his classmates, but he was always isolated with a book. His sweet, mild-mannered disposition left him under the radar, so the teachers didn't pay attention to his developmental delays or deficits.

I made excuses for LM's language and his social disengagement: "Some boys take longer" or "He's 'an only' so he's always under me." I knew I was in denial, but I was afraid, ashamed and fearful of the truth in spite of what the pediatrician said. "Dear _______: Don't worry. I don't want to be ashamed of my son. I'm sorry, LM. Lord, help me."

One evening, while reading to LM, he began repeating what I said—just out of the blue! Here's how it went:

Me: "Good Night Moon"

LM: "Good Night Moon"
Me: "You like the book, Loumike?"
LM: "You like the book, Loumike?"
Me: "Oh my goodness."
LM: "Oh my goodness."

He looked at me and smiled. I looked at back at him and tried to hold back my tears.
Me: "Good boy, Loumike."
LM: "Good boy, Loumike."

"Dear _______: Don't worry. If he can repeat, then he can speak...but this is not normal."

The specialist came to our house to evaluate LM. After fifteen minutes he announced: "HE'S PPD-NOS."
"What?"
"MILD AUTISM."

Autism is a developmental disorder that appears in the first three years of life, and affects the brain's normal development of social and communication skills. Autism Spectrum Disorder (ASD) ranges from mild to severe.

Emotions raced through my mind, body and soul, almost causing hysteria...anger, profound sadness, fear, and back to anger. Why me? I did everything right. I was a Christian. I waited for a mate. I prayed and I was faithful. I just could not believe this was happening to us—to me! Even after the diagnosis, I could not bring myself to say the word "autism." I stuck with saying, "He has a speech delay." I was lying because I was ashamed...of myself...of my own son! I thought that prayer would make it "go away" and that God would heal him since I was a woman of faith. But now, I blamed myself for this terrible label now draped around my son's life. "Dear _______: Don't worry. Help me to love my son despite this label. Help me let go and let God."

Suddenly, a drive of determination arose in me. Immediately, I went from feeling sorry for myself to fighting for my son's life…pushing for LM to receive intense speech therapy…and it worked! We witnessed a gradual blossoming in his development. He began speaking clearly and answering appropriately. He also loved being read to and loved carrying a book under his arm. Socially, he was a bit shy, but that was okay; he was verbal and moving in the right direction. When the whisper of "Thankful" spoke to me, I started an "LM" file on my computer. I began it with: "Dear Son. We love you. We are thankful that God brought you into our lives. Mommy adores you and knows that God made you special."

To watch LM's progression over the last four years has been extremely rewarding. I've stopped blaming myself, because God never makes mistakes. It has been an emotional upheaval, but seeing my letters transform from "Dear _______: Why?" to "Dear _______: Don't worry." to "Dear Son," has shown the growth through my experiences and, ultimately, my healing. Those concrete words gave way to seeing truth. Through my writing, I realized that it was not about me, but about my son and what I needed to do for him. Wow! I was free…like a cool autumn breeze. I had my breakthrough, and now, I am not ashamed to say, "My son has mild autism." LM has a special need, but not in a negative sense—he is special in the sweetest sense of the word.

Our six-year-old, energetic, boy is progressing daily. While life is not "perfect" for him, nor for us as his parents, we would not have him any other way. Now in kindergarten,

Loumike has transitioned from a special needs preschool into our neighborhood public school where his academic skills are on a first grade level. Socially, he is a bit "quirky," but he has friends and enjoys his life at home, church and school. Don't get me wrong…life on the autistic spectrum is challenging, but God has entrusted Loumike to us…and we happily accept the blessing.

Just as Loumike continues to receive speech therapy, I continue my therapy through journaling. It helps me see past the mask and allows my truth to come to surface. "Seeing" my authenticity in print brings me closer to my healing. Today, as a family, we are more happy, hopeful and prayerful than ever before; and through the good and not so good, my writing will always be my outlet:
"Dear _______:"

FAMILY LIES

Kisha Emanuel-Durrell

When I was a little girl, I lived with my mom and my siblings. We were a happy family. On weekends, I would visit my father, who would take me to his great aunt's house instead of taking me home with him. It wasn't until I was grown that I discovered that I was actually supposed to go home with him. My mother would ask how my weekend was and I would tell her it was fine. At that time, I didn't know that she assumed I was spending the whole weekend with my dad.

I don't recall when this lie with my father began, but I was nine years old when it ended. I went to visit my father's aunt that weekend as usual, but my mom fell ill. No one told me about this, but I just felt it in my spirit. I wanted to go home. I had called the house several times and no one answered. That was definitely strange, because my mom or someone else always answered the phone.

When I told my aunt that I wanted to go home, she called my father. When we arrived home, it was like a dark nightmare. No one was around. Mom was not home and none of my siblings were anywhere around. I searched and searched—looking for someone to tell me where my mom was, while my dad just sat in the car peering through the window.

I ran from house to house, finding no one home. Suddenly, I thought to ask Ms. Anna. She was always home. I ran up her stairs and knocked on the door. After what seemed like an eternity, she finally answered.

"Do you know where my mom is?" I asked.

She said, "Baby, your mom is dead."

I could feel my heart fall through the floor. I turned to run down the stairs, and as I reached the porch, I tripped and fell down the last four steps. I was in pain—sure that I had broken something; but the pain in my heart hurt more than any physical pain I was experiencing.

As I lay there crying, my father finally began to walk toward me. Just then, a car pulled up. It was my family. My Aunt Emma came to lift me up from the ground. I couldn't walk. I had indeed broken my leg. My dad didn't say a word. He slowly got back into his car and drove off. I was rushed to the hospital, my leg was put in a cast, and I was given crutches.

That weekend was busy. My family spent the entire time getting ready for mom's funeral…and for our moving to New York with my mom's sister. She was willing to take care of five children—an honorable decision since her children were all grown. It was a comfort that at least our family would still be together.

The day of the funeral was very emotional for me, but even more for my siblings. At age nine, I had to come to the realization that my mother would always live in my heart and that she would want me to keep living. My relationship with God helped me come to this conclusion. I knew that she is with the Father and in a better place. Yes, I will miss her, but one day we will be together.

Living in New York was great. It was like living with mom because she is my mom's twin. They really didn't look alike, but they had similar parenting skills, which made life there great. But one day, something changed. My aunt got a letter from my dad. He wanted his two children, me and my brother. There was nothing she could do since my mom didn't have a living will and he was our biological parent.

Being forced to leave this secure home at age eleven was a nightmare that I was not ready to face. How could he tear me away from my siblings? Why would he do this? Living at my father's home was like taking a step into hell. There were more than 14 people living under his roof at any given time. I did not have a bed to sleep in and my step-mother was not too happy about us being there…and I soon found out that dad was an alcoholic and was rarely sober. My stepmother's kids were bad. They fought a lot, throwing furniture and putting holes in the walls. Eating was a luxury for me. If there was anything left, I was allowed to have it. With so many people in the house, I found lunch at school to be my food source.

My brother fell into their lifestyle right away. I, on the other hand, chose to do what was right. I did not participate in the fights and immoral behavior.

I ran away many times and slept in the basement of the local Catholic Church. I would sneak into the church (the doors were open most of the time back then) and hide until they locked up. I often did not eat because I had no food or money to buy food. I just wanted to be safe. I wanted to tell someone about my predicament, but who would believe me? I was just a child.

I would return home around 6 a.m.—just in time to get ready for school. Sometimes, when I ran away, I had to sleep outside in the bushes. I hated being at my dad's house. I never got a Christmas present, clothes, or shoes. I remember once having to put cardboard in my shoes to cover up the holes. At 13, I was babysitting around the community to make money for shoes, clothes, and having my hair done. But they liked my brother, so he did not have these issues.

One day, I answered an ad in the paper and began babysitting two kids. Within months, I was asked to become a live-in nanny. I asked my dad if I could accept the offer…he asked if I could leave that night. I packed my little suitcase and called a cab. As the cab rolled down the street, my prayer was, "Lord, please never let me have to knock on his door again."

In the days ahead, I chose to connect with peers who came from wholesome families and had two-parent homes. I wanted to glean all I could from these families. Their parents never knew it at the time, but they showed me how to dress like a lady and make sure my words were honorable. They taught me how important it is to get an education. I owe so much to these families. Today, I remain friends with Gail, Barbara, Kim, and Winifred. I wanted to make my mom proud of me as I was growing up; and as I got closer to God, I wanted to please Him more.

Since that time, I have never returned to my dad's house. I heard horrible things about what went on there and I thanked God that He had saved me from that situation. My brother ultimately spent many years in jail; and my step-mother's kids had a rough life of drugs, teen pregnancy and drinking—and their children followed in their footsteps in a life of earthly torment.

Today, I give honor only to my mom for the way I am now. When we were kids, she taught us morals…and she taught us about God. I continue to hold fast to those truths today. "Family" is the one who does the will of the Father.

AN ANSWERED PRAYER

Cynthia Moore

I was 27 years old…pregnant and had a 7-year-old. I was homeless…separated from my husband…sitting at the bus stop wondering what my next move was going to be. At night, I stayed at a 24-hour coffee shop, and with the few pennies in my pocket, I bought coffee. During the day, I sat at the bus stop…as if I were waiting for the bus.

I remember it being a warm, sunny day. I was wearing shades to hide the tears of my broken heart. I never saw myself separated from my husband. I was deeply in love with him. Suddenly, someone pulled up in a white car and called out my name. I looked in the car and saw an old friend inside. I smiled as she asked if I needed a lift.

"Where are you going?" she asked.

I got in the car and we talked for hours as she ran errands. Near the end of the day, she asked me again where I was going. I told her what I was facing at the time…that I was homeless…that I had a son at my mother-in-law's home that I wanted to stay with me. She drove to the side of the road and stopped the car. She embraced me and said, "I have a home big enough for you and your children. You can come stay with me."

She did indeed have a beautiful, roomy home. However, after being married, I had forgotten how "living the single life" was; and since my friend lived a single life, I decided this may not be the best place for my children and me. I moved back in with my mother. My mother had always told me that marriage is not a revolving door; and because I had left my husband several times before, I should stay and work on my marriage. So in order to stay with her, I had to lie.

I got my son back, but when Sunday evening came, I did not know what to tell my mother. I had promised her that I would go back home on Monday. But early Monday morning, a knock came at my mother's door. I had been served with divorce papers. As I read the papers, my knees weakened and I fell into my mother's arms and began to cry. She embraced me and told me that everything would be okay.

Two weeks later, I received a notice from the court stating that my husband wanted custody of our son. By November 30th, I had to show that I had a suitable place for my children and me to live. My mother had a one-bedroom apartment…and it was infested. So, I had two months to find a place. I wanted to get a job, but by now I was already six and a half months pregnant. As I sat at my mother's home, I began to pray. I made a bold request to God. I asked Him for a house, but then I thought that while I'm asking for the things I need, why not ask for all the things I need? I prayed for just that.

Later that day, my sister came to visit. I told her about my prayer and showed her that I had written it and put it in my Bible. She laughed so hard that tears rolled from her eyes and she asked sarcastically, "You really believe that God is going to answer this prayer?" I looked her straight in her eyes and, with confidence, I said, "He's going to answer my prayer." Two weeks later, I found myself staying with that very same sister.

Months passed quickly and before I knew it, November 29th had come. Early that morning, I had begun labor. My sister had joked that if I went into labor while I was with her, she was going to sit me on the porch. Surprisingly, she did just that. She wrapped me up with blankets and gave me my hospital bag.

While I sat on a crate, my sister called her friend to come get me. Her friend escorted me to the car, but then went into the house to exchange choice words with my sister.

Just before we got to the hospital, I told her about my situation and how I needed a place to stay. Excitedly, she told me about a friend who had an empty place where I could stay. I explained that I didn't really have much money, but she was certain something could be worked out.

I had a beautiful baby girl on November 30th. When I called the lady about the empty home, she had already been told about me and my needs. I explained to her that I didn't have any money, and she told me to just move in and we would work things out later.

I didn't know it, but my brother, whom I hadn't seen in over four years, was in town...and my sister had given my new house keys to my brother. So when I got to the home with my beautiful baby girl and my son, my eyes lit up and I smiled. My brother was there! He took my baby and my son as I walked in awe through the house. There was a living room and dining room set, with a beautiful china cabinet. I went to the kitchen and there was a kitchen table with all necessary appliances. The refrigerator and cabinets were filled with food. I ran up the stairs. There were three bedrooms…with beds in them, and in the larger room was a baby's bed already set up and ready to use.

But these things hadn't come from my brother or sister. When the former tenant passed away, the owner had left everything just as it was. The former tenant had just had a new grandbaby, which is why the baby bed was there.

I am 61 years old today. That prayer and many other prayers have been answered in my life. I believe that, if you really believe, you shall receive according to God's will…and His will is that all of your needs be met. So, know that God is mindful of you, and your prayers, you're your needs, and even desires, shall be answered.

WHICH WAY OUT

Rev. Helene M. Walker

The best way to begin my story is to describe a meal that has an ingredient missing. Maybe there is not enough sugar or salt in the food and it doesn't taste quite right. You taste the food to see what's missing but you just can't figure it out. There just seems to be something missing in the dish being prepared. You may even have someone else taste the food for their opinion, and after a few more tastes and adjustments of the ingredients, you finally get it just right. Like a meal with a missing ingredient, that missing ingredient in my life was love. I looked to people for the kind of love that only God can give.

The story of my life begins in a small town—a town where everybody knows everyone. There was one post office, one movie theater and no hospital. Most of the people had come from the south and had little education. My childhood years were spent in the housing projects of this small town. I am the oldest child of five children and my mother, who was a single mom, expected me to be an example to my younger brothers and sisters. I didn't always accept this, but I learned to cope.

There wasn't much to boast about in our small town, but we had a feeling of "oneness" in our community. Everybody was "family." Most of us were related somehow; and even if we weren't related, it felt like we were. There were a lot of "big mama" houses—places you went that felt like home. The children had good clean healthy fun outdoors. We played jump rope, jacks, hide-n-go-seek, two square, four squares, baseball, volley ball and many other outdoor games—playing outside for hours. The neighbors had gardens and fruit trees in their yards and we would eat outside when we were hungry instead of going into the house for food. The ice cream truck—the "Good Humor" truck—rode all over the neighborhood, selling ice cream and popsicles; and there was always an uncle or aunt, a big brother or big sister, or someone to buy something for you from the "Good Humor" man. There was a special tune that played loudly; and even if you were in the house, you still could hear that tune. It had kids running after the truck from all over the neighborhood to get that special treat.

As I grew into adulthood, things became more complicated; and my feeling of security in this small community of "oneness" was not so simple anymore. When you're a child, there are many things that you just don't notice. On the surface, everything seems just fine. Adults try to hide things from children to protect them; but sooner or later, everything is revealed. I learned the stark reality of living in poverty and living in housing projects. Project life was all I knew, and I didn't know my way out. As I grew older, my eyes were opened to the "sin problems" in my family and in the neighborhood. I was hurt and I was in pain; but I was taught to stay in a "child's place" and don't ask questions. So I withdrew within myself. It's odd how we can be so blind to the sin all around us, and when we do realize the sin problem, we quietly turn our heads. I began to realize we were poor and that the people I loved the most had sin problems. My eyes were opened to the fact that police officers were sometimes the biggest crooks and that preachers can sometimes be the biggest sinners. I was crushed, and it seemed like there was no way out of this dark sinful world.

I fell into the arms of my teenage boyfriend for that sense of security I needed. We were always together; he was my friend. He walked me home from school and protected me from the bullies. We talked about everything and anything for hours. We were in love…so I thought. I felt safe with him, but I had mistaken that feeling of false security for love.

I became pregnant too soon and we got married. He joined the army and sent for me and the baby. We lived together in Germany for about 16 months. But things didn't go so well there. I found out he was a drug user. He abused me mentally and physically…and destroyed my passport so that I could not leave the country. He also abused our small baby and made us prisoners in our own home. There were times when I had no food, no money and no friends. I lived in constant fear. I remember feeding my baby sugar water in his bottle because there was nothing else to give him. I remember knocking on the Germans' doors, asking for food to eat. I remember burning our clothes in a room heater to keep warm. My world had become even darker…darker than the one I had known in the projects. I thought I had escaped the reality of the sinful lives of people in my small childhood town, but I only became trapped in a failing marriage with no way out. We were in a foreign country…far away from family and friends. My only way out was to end my life…so I thought. I failed at trying to take my life—not once, but twice, first as a teenager in the projects and again in Germany. The world seemed like a sinful dark place with no way out.

But one day, when I was in the hallway at the door of my apartment with my baby in my arms, I heard a voice that said to me, "Go Home." I heard two simple words—"Go Home." I believed it was the voice of God; and with the help of some strangers who were also in that country serving in the military, I managed to go back home.

When I finally arrived back home in the United States, it was difficult to adjust. Believing that divorce is a sin, I tried one more time to make my marriage work. We had two more children and life was okay…but only for a little while. He began to beat me again, and because of the fear that he would kill me if I stayed in the marriage, I divorced him anyway.

I had recurring dreams of being trapped in a large building with the ability to fly. I would fly around the building, trying to find a way out. In my dreams, there was always something there trying to grab me and pull me down, but I would always manage to escape. It was those feelings of being trapped and unloved that lead me to this dark place where I had become a prisoner.

I went back to the church I had attended before I left the country—but this time with a different outlook on life. This time I was bruised and broken. It's amazing how brokenness can bring us closer to God. The pastor made me feel special. He was like the father I never had. In the church, I had found a place where there was a sense of belonging—a place where other broken people were crying to God for help. So I too poured out my heart to God and my life began to get better. I had found a place where there were others like me—who were not accepting sin, but were asking God for help.

As I listened to the sermons and attended Sunday school and Bible classes, I learned how much God loves me. Agape love—that was the missing ingredient that I needed in my life. God had always been there carrying me—I just didn't realize it. My children were growing up in the church and I was growing up in the church as well. We had a church family. God must have known that we cannot always find what we need in our biological families, so He created another family—a family of believers in Christ Jesus. We were blessed as a family of believers who trusted God to deliver us from our sins. I am coming out of bondage; I am being set free; my past is behind me. I'm no longer in that dark place. I'm learning to depend on Him. I have found a way out of that dark place, and I have a joy within me now. I can feel the love of God working in my life. When I look back on my life, I can see how God has guided me out of that dark place where I felt so unloved.

I had looked for love my whole life long and I finally found that love in Christ Jesus. "For God so loved the world that He gave His only begotten Son." Yes, I finally found real love! Yes, Jesus loves me! Yes, Jesus saved me! I still have problems, but I meet them head-on with a different mindset—with a mind that's stayed on Jesus—a mind that believes in Christ. When you know differently, you act differently; and the result is a changed life.

Now that I have complete confidence in Christ, I have begun to make changes in my life. I received a bachelor's degree. I have a good job. I am married again—this time to a man who loves me and does not abuse me. I have raised strong, healthy children who believe in God, and I have grandchildren that I adore. I have become active in leadership roles in the church and in the community. I am living my life for God—teaching, preaching, writing and serving others. My life is very different now. I have learned about all the wonderful gifts God has for me. He promised life abundantly. He promised a heavenly home. He gave us the comfort of the Holy Spirit, and because of what he has already done in our lives, we can forever depend and trust in his promises.

I cried, "Lord Help me!" and he showed me the way out of my loveless situations. Jesus said, "I am the way, the truth and the life." I believe that with all my heart. God's love lifted me and God's love saved me. JESUS IS THE WAY OUT!

JUST BELIEVE

Andrea L. Dudley

Everyone is talking about it…Anthony Robbins, Oprah, Dr. Oz, Bishop T. D. Jakes, Deepak Chopra and Joel Osteen…Buddhist, Catholic, Atheist, Christian and non-Christian…all are examining it.

On every continent of the world people want to know how to go to the next level or how to break through or break out. How to be more! Get more! Do more! There's an innate nagging on the inside of us that keeps prompting us: "You can do better. There's more. Keep striving. Don't settle."

I'm no different—in the fact that I do want more. I want to do more. I want to have more. And it's not so much for me to consume my own fleshly desires, but for me to accomplish or fulfill my purpose on this earth…or at least that's what I tell myself. I don't think I'm greedy for things. I'm not striving for material goods, but I am on a journey of discovery. I am striving to be all that my creator created me to be.

Inside each of us is the potential to do something great. Philosophers, scientists and theologians believe this to be true. Inside of us lies a reservoir of untapped potential.

There are untold numbers of stories about people who have done amazing feats—far exceeding their own expectations. Through insurmountable odds, they were able to rise above defeat, depression and despondency. They tapped into the potential they were born with in order to live their dreams.

I am reminded of a story about Roger Bannister. Just a few decades ago, track-and-field experts proudly declared that no runner could break the four-minute-mile barrier. It was said that a human being couldn't run that distance that fast. "Experts" conducted all types of profound studies to show that it was impossible to beat the four-minute-mile barrier. And for years, they were right—no one ever ran a mile in less than four minutes.

But one day a young man came along who didn't believe the experts' opinions. He didn't dwell on the impossible. He refused to let those negative words form a stronghold in his mind. He began to train—believing he would be able to break that record. Sure enough, he did just that. One day, he finally accomplished his dream and broke the four-minute-mile barrier. The experts said it couldn't be done—but he did it—he made sports history!

We don't have to think for very long before we come up with the names of others who shattered the barriers of limitations.

Barack Obama made history when he became the first African-American president despite the many naysayers who said that it was impossible for him to win the election. This is not a political statement—just a fact.

Madam C.J. Walker became the first African-American female millionaire.

> "I am a woman who came from the cotton fields of the South. From there I was promoted to the washtub. From there I was promoted to the cook kitchen. And from there I promoted myself into the business of

> manufacturing hair goods and preparations….I have built my own factory on my own ground."
> --Madam Walker, National Negro Business League Convention, July 1912

Kathryn Kuhlman's unique abilities to yield to the power of the Holy Spirit, or the untapped potential inside of her, enabled her to see thousands of people healed from all kinds of diseases.

These people all had one thing in common—they believed they could achieve their goal. They believed that, as they yielded themselves to God, they would do great things.

But without faith it is impossible to please him: for he that cometh to God must believe that he is, and that he is a rewarder of them that diligently seek him. –Hebrews 11:6

Between potential and greatness, however, there are challenges—circumstances and situations that threaten to keep us from becoming all that we were created to be.

We live in a world where boundaries are all around us—where people are constantly telling us what we are capable or incapable of doing. They say things like, "It has never been done before" or "No one has ever done it this way"—"You're too dumb to be a lawyer" or "You're too fat to be a doctor." They say…and they say…"You're too dark; no one wants a dark woman." People are always pushing their self-imposed limitations on others.

If you don't know any better, you'll believe the lie. If a person doesn't know that they were born for a reason and that they weren't a "mistake," they muddle through life being kicked around like a football. Well… that is really a different subject…the part about being "kicked around like a football."

But let me digress for a moment. Many people believe that we're the master of our own fate. William Ernest Henley said, "I am the master of my fate: I am the captain of my soul." They believe that whatever circumstances we find ourselves in today--it is a result of the decisions and choices we have made.

I choose to believe that, to a great extent, I am in control of my life. I am responsible for the outcomes of the choices I make. God created me as a free agent—not a robot whose every movement is decided by someone else. But I also realize that the God I serve is sovereign—that he exceeds all authority and power! Many, however, use the sovereignty of God as an excuse to not take responsibility for their own decisions—to not use their God-given authority and power to maximize the potential God created them with. "God is in control," they say, as though they don't have to do anything but sit back on autopilot while life rolls along—just sit back and enjoy the ride. I beg to differ with this thought process.

We are created in the image of God—filled with unlimited potential that, through the enabler, the Holy Spirit, we can have whatever we believe we can have. There is nothing else that God is going to do. We have been given all power and authority here on earth. We simply have to use it. So, no matter what situation or circumstances you may find yourself in, you can get through it. You can rise above it. You can beat it. You can win!

For as he thinks in his heart, so is he. –Proverbs 23:7

In my own personal life I have enjoyed adventures beyond what many people experience…simply because I chose to believe. Here is a case in point:

One evening Michael (my husband) and I were watching the travel channel. It was a special about a place in South Africa called The Sun City Resort. The resort draws thousands of visitors each year to its four hotels, including two five-star hotels: the Palace of the Lost City (which forms part of The Leading Hotels of the World) and The Cascades Hotel. In the television special, they were showing photos of the Palace of the Lost City hotel—the delectable buffet meals, the lush, beautiful landscape, the exquisite rooms and all that the hotel had to offer. Wow…I was mesmerized. I could see myself there. I envisioned myself sitting at one of the pools…relaxing and eating sweet pineapple and dining on meals fit for a queen. I said to my husband, "I want to visit there!" "Impossible," some would say. Well, within one year we were on our way to South Africa to stay in the Palace of the Lost City. That proved to be one of the best trips that we ever made. It was amazing.

So, you see, when I saw that television show, I immediately grabbed hold of what I saw…what I felt. I believed that I could actually visit this place. The power to create and obtain "wealth" is inside of me so I tapped into my God-given imagination and saw myself there…that beautiful place where the rich and famous visit. I could have said, "Oh well, I guess I'll never visit that place. We could never afford it." Well…guess what? We didn't have to pay to stay there nor did we have to pay to get there. It was an all-expense paid vacation! Go figure! This trip was only one of many exotic vacations our family has taken.

Beloved, God has so much more for you. Do you believe it? Can you see it? Can you touch it?

The first thing that you must do is enlarge the territory of your mind. Dream bigger! Take the limits off! Do you realize that the limitations are only in our minds?...our thinking?

I challenge you today to begin a renovation of your mind. Tear down the old-dilapidated frame and structure and start building with a fresh, new foundation…one that can hold the new life-prints you are creating.

Remember—If you can believe it, it's possible!

Author Biographies

Rebecca Bailey

Rebecca Bailey is first and foremost a servant of the Most High GOD. A lifelong Michigan resident, she is a single mother of a wonderful son, Jacob, author of "Someone Else's Diary," a recent graduate with a Bachelor of Science in Business/Communication, and she is currently working to launch Hannah's Heartcry Ministry, an outreach for young, pregnant women in need.

Pastor Kimberly Brown

Affectionately known as Pastor Kim, Kimberly Brown is the wife of a loving husband, Deacon Tony Brown. Together they have six children. She serves as Sr. Pastor of Zion Cathedral of Praise International Ministries in Port Huron, Michigan. The Lord has given Pastor Kim a love for His people and a desire to see people healed and set free from the effects of sin. Pastor Kim is a licensed, Master's Level social worker by profession, and she holds a Certification in Advanced Addiction Counseling. She was blessed of the Lord to found and establish Zoe Counseling and Consulting, Inc.

Judith S. Cooper

Judith Cooper is currently pursuing her doctorate in Management of Nonprofit Organizations from the School of Public Leadership at Capella University. Her dissertation centers on African American professional women who are raising adolescent daughters to become entrepreneurs through transformational leadership. She also has an extensive work history as a professional psychotherapist, and she attained her Master's degree in Pastoral Counseling from Ashland Theological Seminary, counseling individuals, married couples and families.

In 2010, Judith began a happy marriage with Leroi Cooper. Her adult children, Julian (25), Myvretta Joy (22) and Joseph (20) are operating under the anointing in ministry.

Michele Sweeting DeCaro

Hailing from New York City, Michele's distinct, stylish vocals, as well as her powerful testimony, touch the hearts of all who hear her. She attributes her skill in music ministry to the anointing power of the Holy Spirit and the Triune God.

Michele's vocal ministry has afforded her worldwide travel—from New York to Philadelphia—from Oregon to Detroit—from Atlanta to Nashville—from Trinidad to Russia, where she shares her testimony of God's grace in her life through song. Michele's CD, *Center Of My Joy* has netted tremendous response. The CD landed on the ballot for the "Song of The Year" category for both the Stellar and Dove Awards. Michele is equally excited about her sophomore CD, *Lamb of God*, a wonderful collection of songs, reflective of her walk with the Lord.

Michele teaches Literature, Theory and Writing courses at The City College of New York, *Center For Worker Education* (CWE) and is the coordinator of the CWE writing center. Michele feels blessed to serve in ministry alongside her husband, Dr. Louis A. DeCaro, Jr., Pastor of Fellowship Chapel in the Bronx, N.Y., and their "singing" young son, Louis Michael.

Michele's purpose in life is simple: to glorify the name of the One and Only, True and Living Son of GOD…JESUS CHRIST.

Kisha Emanuel-Durrell

Kisha is recently the publisher of a book called "Ten Days," a story of love, hope and family. In her spare time, she enjoys volunteering in the community to give back what God has blessed her with. She loves to spend time with her children and grandchildren—going to the movies and theatre. Kisha looks forward to 2012 being a year of travel, and a year of great and wonderful things. She is a member of Toastmasters International, Women In Touch and Writers Market.

Minister Mary Edwards

Minister Mary Edwards is founder of The Called and Ready Writers, a Christian writers' guild in Detroit. Mary is a book coach, editor and publisher, as well as a motivational speaker. (www.thecalledandreadywriters). She is founder and CEO of Leaves of Gold Consulting. (www.leavesofgoldconsulting.com). Mary has appeared in "Who's Who in Black Detroit" several times, as well as in Black Enterprise magazine and Chicken Soup for the Soul books. Many know Mary Edwards as co-founder of Joy of Jesus Ministries, along with her late husband, Rev. Eddie K. Edwards. She can be reached by calling (313) 492-0149 or by emailing her at leavesofgold.llc@gmail.com.

Zabrina Gordon

Zabrina Gordon currently resides in the Metro Atlanta area. She is a graduate of Oglethorpe University and has a Bachelor's Degree in Organizational Management and Psychology. She and her husband, Derrick Gordon, have been married for eight years. Currently, Zabrina is a member of Hopewell Missionary Baptist Church under the leadership of Bishop William L. Sheals. She currently serves as a Christian Counselor. One of Zabrina's favorite scriptures is Philippians 3:14: *I press on toward the goal to win the prize for which God has called me heavenward in Christ Jesus.*

Linda A. Haywood

Linda Haywood is the author of her autobiography, Does God Really Hear Me When I Cry? A Life Transformed. She is also a Licensed Minister and a Master's level Social Worker in the State of Michigan. She can be reached at thatwriterlady@yahoo.com or learn more by visiting her website at www.thecalledandreadywriters.org.

Rev. Dr. Peninnah M. Kako

Rev. Kako is an anointed teacher of the Word of God and has a great desire to see God's people delivered and set free. She has boldly declared, *"The Spirit of the Lord is upon me, because he hath anointed me to preach the gospel to the poor..."* (Luke 4:18-19 KJV). She is a co-pastor at Global Vision Center Ministries in Milwaukee, Wisconsin, together with her husband, Rev. John M. Kako. She is a proud mother of two God-fearing sons, Joseph (22) and Paul (21).

Pastor O. Agnes Kgasoe

Pastor Kgasoe is founder of Kingdom Children's Ministries and Co-Founder and President of Youth Link. Her heart's desire is for children and young people to know Jesus Christ as their personal Saviour. Each year, she hosts many seminars and youth camps.

"Pastor Aggy" and her husband are the founders of Word of Hope International Ministries in Mabopane, Pretoria. She is an ordained pastor, an international speaker and a life coach.

She received her Bachelor of Arts Degree from Vista University and Bachelor of Arts Honours from University of Pretoria, South Africa.

She has been married to Pastor Solofelang Kgasoe for 25 years, and she is the mother of two daughters, Reitumetse and Reneilwe.

To contact Agnes, call: +27 12 525 1270/+27 82 958 6454 or email her at akgasoe@gmail.com

Faith Larkins

Faith Larkins was born and raised in Detroit, Michigan, and is the youngest of four sisters. Faith has been employed with the State of Michigan for over twenty years. She is a member of Living Bread Ministries in Redford, Michigan, where she actively participates in the Praise and Worship Team, the Prophetic Team, the Deliverance Team, and also serves as the head of Security. Her desire is simply to live out God's plan for her life.

Being an author in this book represents a new leg of her long but fruitful journey. God has been faithful to open the doors to her destiny; and this is one of the first of those Godly opportunities. Her prayer is that, when people read her story, they will be blessed and encouraged. With God, ALL things are possible…if you have faith and believe!! To God be the glory! Amen!

Amy J. Meyer-Johnson

Amy Meyer-Johnson was born and raised in Michigan City, Indiana. She is the mother of six children and an administrative professional in the Graduate School of Marquette University in Milwaukee, Wisconsin. In her spare time, Amy enjoys reading, writing, singing, cross stitch and cooking. This publication in this book is an excerpt from a novel in progress, her first attempt at professional writing.

Cynthia Moore

A native of Detroit, Cynthia Moore is a proud mother and grandmother. Her children and grandchildren are her cherished gifts from God. Cynthia is founder of Women In Touch, a non-profit organization that helps women and children who are victims of domestic violence, substance abuse and homelessness. Cynthia spends many hours "giving back" in the community. Her spare time is spent writing and producing stage plays and comedy shows. Cynthia's favorite quote is: "You can do all things through Christ Jesus."

Caroline D. Parker

Caroline Parker was born in Detroit and raised in Inkster, Michigan. She graduated from Inkster High School and received her bachelor's degree from The University of Michigan in Ann Arbor. While at UM, she won the Hopwood Award for Essay Writing. She earned her Masters of Public Administration degree in Political Science from Eastern Michigan University. Caroline has a passion for science fiction movies, good books, music, screenwriting and drama. She also attended a voiceover class at the Dramatic Arts Studio in Ferndale, Michigan, and wants to pursue a career in inspirational voiceover narration.

Evangelist Valerie M. Robinson

Valerie accepted the Lord as her personal savior at the age of 18 and has served in multiple ministerial capacities. Valerie is married to Melvin G. Robinson and they have one daughter, Chelsea Glenn Robinson.

Valerie attends Consuming Fire Christian Center in Westland, Michigan, under the leadership of Senior Pastor Keith Hudson and Co-Pastor Bernadette Hudson. She is an ordained Minister and Chaplain and has ministered in various venues throughout the United States and Canada.

Valerie is already a published author in the internationally released "Talitha Cumi" Book Series with her story entitled "Have Faith in God."

Carolyn Solomon

Carolyn graduated from Northern High in Detroit, Michigan, and worked on their student paper. She entered a short story writing contest offered by Ingenue Magazine and won first prize.

After 2 ½ years at St. Mary's in Nauvoo, Illinois, Carolyn left the convent and met her husband, whom she married 51 years ago. They have 3 children, 9 grandchildren and 4 great-grandchildren.

Carolyn is the author of Thirsting Hearts, Entanglements, Amazing Grace and Loving Is Forgiving. She won "honorable mention" for I Am Found, presented in Ebony Magazine's 2003 issue.

Rev. Helene M. Walker

Rev. Walker serves as a Licensed Associate Minister, Sunday School Teacher, and Missionary Leader at Mt. Zion Missionary Baptist Church in Ecorse, Michigan. She also serves as Chaplain at the Ford Motor Company Engine Plant and is a volunteer shepherd at Oakwood Rehabilitation/Skilled Nursing Center, both in Dearborn Michigan. Helene has a Bachelor's Degree in Religious Studies from Heritage College/Seminary in Ontario, Canada. She is an associated writer for "He Reigns" Gospel Magazine in Kalamazoo, Michigan. She is married to her husband Karlos, and they are proud parents and grandparents. Her spiritual mission is to make disciples according to Matthew 28:19-20.

Linda Jo White

Linda is a Kingdom of God-seeking, world-changing, loving wife and joyful mother who is blessed to fulfill the purpose for which she was created. While she wears many hats during the course of the day and week, one of her favorites is that of "Kingdom Cheerleader." The lifestyle freedoms she enjoys as a result of managing the family business affords her the privilege of being able to serve her family, friends, employees, customers, neighbors, church brothers and sisters and those God places in her path with a grateful heart and to the glory of God.

Apostle Londen Winters

In 1994, God told Apostle Londen Winters: "Go and find my lost sheep, my daughters, and heal them." Londen was ordained in 1995 and she founded Londen Winters Ministries, a healing, deliverance and teaching ministry for hurting souls.

Among the many miracles witnessed during Londen Winters services are recovery from life-threatening diseases, removal of breast and spinal tumors, and the raising of the afflicted from their sickbeds.

Londen has a degree in mental health with a certificate in drug rehabilitation counseling. She has a ministry in Pakistan and is the overseer of Wailing Women in Detroit.

New Life in Christ

"For God so loved the world
that he gave his one and only Son,
that whoever believes in him shall not perish
but have eternal life."
-John 3:16 New International Version

We hope that you have been blessed by **It's Possible: Living Beyond Limitations!** Perhaps you are not Born Again and want to receive Christ today! You can do it right now, no matter where you are.

Pray this simple prayer…

"Father, I come to you in the Name of Jesus. I repent of my sins and ask you to come into my heart. I know that I need you and that you love and care for me. Cleanse me by your blood. Renew my mind and deliver me from all habits and thoughts that are contrary to you and your Word. I commit my life to you now and I thank you that I have received eternal life. Thank you for dying on the cross for me. In Jesus' name I pray. Amen."

You are now a Christian! Tell somebody!

- Pray and ask the Lord to help you find a good Bible-teaching, Spirit-filled church.
- Read your Bible every day!
- Talk to God through prayer on a daily basis.
- Ask Him to fill you with the Holy Spirit.

About Habakkuk Publishing

Habakkuk Publishing (HP):
a global publishing company that publishes your vision

We will take your manuscript and transform it into a book! We provide the services of editing, proofreading, printing, rewrites and more!

If you are interested in beginning the exciting journey of becoming a published author, let us help you. We believe in empowering authors so that they have the confidence and resources to succeed.

We are always looking for inspirational, motivational, true stories of how one has been able to rise above the challenging obstacles, hindrances and setbacks of life.

For the specifications and information on how to submit an article, please be sure to visit our website at: www.globalempact.org/habakkuk_publishing.

For additional information, please contact:
Andrea L. Dudley, 734.772.2079 or
habakkukstories@yahoo.com

www.globalempact.org

Other anthologies published by

Habakkuk Publishing

TALITHA CUMI:
MOTHERS OF THE NATIONS ARISE!

TALITHA CUMI:
DAMSEL I SAY UNTO THEE ARISE!

TALITHA CUMI: DAUGHTERS ARISE!

TALITHA CUMI:
MOTHERS & DAUGHTERS ARISE

TALITHA CUMI: GET UP GIRL

Game On: Becoming a Man who Pleases God

Order your copies today!

GLOBAL E.M.P.A.C.T

INTERNATIONAL

CONTACT INFORMATION

http://www.globalempact.org

Booking information for:
ANDREA L. DUDLEY, B.S, M.A.
Entrepreneur—Life & Family Coach

Entrepreneur, Life Coach, Radio Talk Show Host, CEO of Habakkuk Publishing, Andrea L. Dudley, is available to speak at your church, conference, retreats, or company event.

Andrea enjoys speaking to a variety of audiences and speaks on subjects from leadership development, to maximizing your potential, to breaking barriers and boundaries. Her witty, fun delivery challenges her audience to examine themselves and to "reach higher."

Andrea can be contacted at the following email address: habakkukstories@yahoo.com. Be sure to visit her website at www.globalempact.org.